Employment/ Unemployment and Earnings Statistics

A Guide to Locating Data in U.S. Documents

John M. Ross

The Scarecrow Press, Inc.
Lanham, Md., & London

SCARECROW PRESS, INC.

Published in the United States of America
by Scarecrow Press, Inc.
4720 Boston Way
Lanham, Maryland 20706

4 Pleydell Gardens, Folkestone
Kent CT20 2DN, England

British Cataloguing-in-Publication Information Available

Library of Congress Cataloging-in-Publication Data

Ross, John M. (John Murray)
Employment/unemployment and earnings statistics in U.S. documents :
a guide to locating data in U.S. documents / by John M. Ross.
p. cm.
Includes bibliographical references and index.
1. Labor market—United States—Statistics—Bibliography. 2.
Unemployment—United States—Statistics—Bibliography. 3. Wages—
United States—Statistics—Bibliography. 4. Labor market—United States—
Statitistical services. 5. Unemployment—United States—Statistical services.
6. Wages—United States—Statistical services. I. Title.
Z7164.L1R729 1996 [HD5724] 016.33112'0973—dc20 95–46965 CIP

ISBN 0-8108-3099-X (cloth : alk. paper)

Printed in the United States of America

☉™ The paper used in this publication meets the minimum requirements of
American National Standard for Information Sciences—Permanence of
Paper for Printed Library Materials, ANSI Z39.48–1984.

Contents

Part 2

READY-REFERENCE GUIDE

Part 3

APPENDICES

Acknowledgments

I wish to express my deepest appreciation to Linda Koike, library government publications assistant, California State University, Los Angeles, for her computer assistance, and to Eileen Utake for her assistance here also.

I would also very much like to thank Mark Dodge, the prepress editor.

Introduction

This publication serves as a time-saving source for locating employment/unemployment and personal income/earnings data on the U.S. labor force from the multitude of documents issued by the U.S. government. It represents the first attempt to bring together in a single source a reference tool that provides significant data on this subject. It also represents the first attempt at analyzing the contents of the many comprehensive studies on labor statistics in the form of a ready-reference guide.

Bibliography

This book is in two parts: the bibliography and the ready-reference guide. The bibliography covers all documents which provide keynote statistics on the labor force, including those cited in the ready-reference guide. Although most of the references here are publications of the Bureau of Labor Statistics and the Bureau of the Census, also included are the many documents of other government bureaus, offices, commissions, and committees. To avoid becoming quickly obsolete or dated, this bibliography covers only documents of a serial nature, either regular or irregular, and other publications that are updated or revised on an ongoing basis. Documents which are one-time or conclusive studies, with no updates or revisions forthcoming, are omitted from this publication.

The bibliography is divided into three sections. Chapter one refers to comprehensive reports which all contain general data including employment, unemployment, and income/earnings. The comprehensive reports (I.1-20) are cited in both sections of the ready-reference guide. Chapters two through five consider the reports which contain information on employment and unemployment, and chapters six through eight cover material on income and earnings.

The entries are arranged under subject by frequency of publication (weekly, monthly, annual, etc.), then alphabetically within each frequency, with the irregularly published documents appearing at the end of each group.

Each citation or reference contains a complete bibliographic entry, a short description of the document, and the Superintendent of Documents classification number, commonly referred to as the SuDocs number. Since all entries are of a serial nature, or are frequently revised, only the SuDocs number for the latest report or edition is given. If the SuDocs number has changed, locating classification numbers for earlier reports can be found through the standard document indexes or through the assistance of the documents librarian.

The annotations describe briefly the documents' coverage on employment/unemployment and/or income/earnings. Other data cited in these publications generally are not noted. Annotations for those titles which appear in the ready-reference guide, including most comprehensive reports, do not detail what areas of labor force subjects they cover, e.g., national, state, local, etc., because such information can be found through the ready-reference guide. Documents which do not appear in the ready-reference guide are more fully described. Documents cited in the ready-reference guide, are identified by the acronym RRG after the citation. The references which appear in only one guide are identified RRG 1 or RRG 2. The comprehensive reports which appear in both guides indicate RRG 1-2.

Ready-Reference Guide

The ready-reference guide, as the title suggests, serves as a quick access to labor force data. While there are copious data published on the labor force, and its statistics are repeated in many publications of the Bureau of Labor Statistics and the Census Bureau, not to mention those of other agencies, an attempt to identify which one (or ones) to study can often be timeconsuming, aggravating, and sometimes, in the end, disappointing. It is therefore the purpose of this guide to assist the user expeditiously through the maze of documents on the U.S. labor force.

The ready-reference guide refers to those publications on employment/unemployment and/or income/earnings which cover these topics generally such as all or most geographical areas, races, and industries. It does not include documents confined to a specific industry or population group. Data of that nature will be found in the bibliography.

For purposes of organization, the ready-reference guide is divided into two parts: employment/unemployment, and income/earnings. The document titles are listed in the left column and the subject breakdowns appear along the top. There are four geographic breakdowns with each division subdivided by age/sex/race and Hispanic origin. The remaining subject breakdowns are congressional district, zip code, major industry, detailed industry, major occupation, detailed occupation, and foreign countries.[*] Like the bibliography, titles are arranged by frequency of publication, then alphabetically within each frequency. The frequency is indicated immediately after the title. This is followed by the location number for the document citation in the bibliography which gives the complete bibliographic entry, a short description of the document, and the Superintendent of Documents (Sudocs) classification number. The user is advised to supplement the ready-reference guide by surveying the bibliography for reports on specific industries, specific population groups, and other subject areas covering the labor force.

Subject Indices

The extensive subject index provides an additional source to guide the user through the contents of this publication. Subject headings used in the index and the bibliography are based on the *Library of*

---

[*] Labor force data on foreign countries often cannot easily be found—especially for third-world countries. Such materials are included here—because they are readily available in various U.S. documents.

Congress subject headings, 15th ed., and the subject headings in the *Monthly catalog*.

For the most part, comprehensive reports (I.1-20) are not given a detailed analysis in the subject index as they are already analyzed in the ready-reference guide; however, there are two exceptions: the *Census tracts* (I.8) and the *Foreign labor trends* (I.24). These two publications consist of a series of separately published titles, each covering a specific area or country. A subject entry for each of these titles appears in the subject index, as the ready-reference guide does not cover documents on a specific topic.

Bibliographic Sources

The principal sources used to compile this bibliography were the *American statistics index*, the *Congressional information service*, the *Marcive GPO CAT/PAC ... CD ROM version catalog of government publications*, and the *Monthly catalog*. Also consulted, especially for recent references, were the daily depository shipping lists received from the Superintendent of Documents at the University Library, California State University, Los Angeles.

In conclusion, this is not an exhaustive bibliography of government reports covering the area of employment/unemployment and earnings/income. While all relevant Census Bureau and Bureau of Labor Statistics publications of a continuing nature are included, it does not cover all separately published reports on each occupation and industry. Representative samples released on each industry and occupation, however, are provided. Data on most industries and occupations can be found in many of the comprehensive reports of these two agencies (see ready-reference guide for coverage). While this is not a comprehensive bibliography, it does serve as a basic reference for researching employment/unemployment and earnings, and, consequently, should prove a valuable time saver for both the experienced searcher and the novice in exploring this area.

Part 1

Bibliography

Chapter One

Comprehensive Reports on Employment/Unemployment and Income/Earnings Data

Periodicals

I.1.   *Employment and earnings*. BLS. L 2.41/2:v./no. monthly. RRG 1-2.

The most comprehensive and current source on labor force statistics. Provides data on employment, unemployment, hours, and earnings for the United States as a whole, for individual states, and for more than 200 local areas. Data are from the Current Population Survey[1] of households and from the Current Employment Survey[2] of nonagricultural establishments. Revised establishment data are cumulated in the annual publication, *Supplement to employment and earnings* (I.6).

I.2.   *The Employment situation*. BLS. L 2.53/2:(date) monthly. RRG 1-2.

Monthly press release giving current U.S. labor force statistics. Statistics are from the Current Population Survey[1] (household survey) and the Current Employment Survey[2] (establishment survey).

I.3.   *Monthly labor review*. BLS. L 2.6:v./no. monthly. RRG 1-2. Articles on labor force, wages, prices, productivity, economic growth, and occupational injuries and illnesses. Regular features include a review of developments in industrial relations, book reviews, and current labor statistics, including employment/unemployment and earnings, and employment/unemployment in ten major industrial countries.

Annuals, Biennials, etc.

I.4.   *Employment and wages, annual averages.* BLS. L 2.104/2:yr. annual. RRG 1-2.

Presents complete account of employment and wages for workers covered by unemployment insurance programs in the 50 states and the District of Columbia. For private industry, gives employment and wage statistics by major and detailed industry. For government, gives employment and wage statistics by selected industry for state, local, and federal government.

I.5.   *Statistical abstract of the United States.* Census Bureau. C 3.134:yr. annual. RRG 1-2.

This reference book is the standard summary of statistics on the social, political, and economic organization of the United States. Each edition contains a section, "Labor force, employment, and earnings." Also contains sections: "State and local government finances and employment," "Federal government finances and employment," and "Employment and unemployment" in the ten major industrial countries. *Statistical abstract* also available on CD-ROM: C 3.134/7:yr.

I.6.   *Supplement to Employment and earnings, revised establishment data.* BLS. L 2.41/2-2:yr. annual. RRG 1-2.

Gives primarily annual update of employment, hours, and earnings data by detailed industry of nonagricultural establishments. Supplements the historical publication *Employment, hours and earnings, United States* (I.17). State and local area data are available in a companion volume, *Employment hours and earnings, states and areas* (I.16). Current data appears in the monthly *Employment and earnings* (I.1).

I.7.   *U.S.A. counties, a Statistical abstract supplement.* Census Bureau. C 3.134/6:Un 3/yr./CD. annual. RRG 1-2.

Issued in compact disc, this 1992 release is the first edition of *U.S.A. Counties*. Provides population, housing, social, and economic statistics (including employment/unemployment and earnings) for the last ten years for the U.S., states, and counties, also employment statistics for counties by major industry and major occupation.

I.8.   *Census of population and housing. Population and housing characteristics for census tracts and block numbering areas.* Census Bureau. C 3.223/11:990 CPH-3-no. decennial. RRG 1-2.

Released every ten years with the decennial census, the *Tracts* give detailed statistics on population and housing by tracts for MSAs, states, selected counties, selected places of 10,000 or more population, and other tracted areas. Separate reports for each MSA and state, Puerto Rico, and the Virgin Islands, with two parts for each report: statistics and maps. Census tract reports for metropolitan areas are numbered as follows:

Area	Report No.
Abilene, TX MSA	*58*
Aguadilla, PR MSA	*59*
Albany, GA MSA	*60*
Albany-Schenectady-Troy, NY MSA	*61*
Albuquerque, NM MSA	*62*
Alexandria, LA MSA	*63*
Allentown-Bethlehem-Easton, PA-NJ MSA	*64*
Altoona, PA MSA	*65*
Amarillo, TX MSA	*66*
Anchorage, AK MSA	*67*
Anderson, IN MSA	*68*
Anderson, SC MSA	*69*
Anniston, AL MSA	*70*
.Appleton-Oshkosh-Neenah, WI MSA	*71*
Arecibo, PR MSA	*72*
Asheville, NC MSA	*73*

Area	Report No.
Wheeling, WV-OH MSA	*336*
Wichita, KS MSA	*337*
Wichita Falls, TX MSA	*338*
Williamsport, PA MSA	*339*
Wilmington, NC MSA	*340*
Worcester, MA MSA	*341*
Yakima, WA MSA	*342*
York, PA MSA	*343*
Youngstown-Warren, OH MSA	*344*
Yuba City, CA MSA	*345*
Yuma, AZ MSA	*346*

I.9. *Census of population and housing. Population and housing characteristics for congressional districts.* Census Bureau. C 3.223/20:990 CPH-4-no. decennial. RRG 1-2.

One report for each state and the District of Columbia, giving population and housing data for congressional districts, and within CDs for counties, places of 10,000 or more inhabitants, and for MCDs (minor civil divisions) of 10,000 or more inhabitants in selected states within each congressional district. Labor force characteristics for state and congressional district include employment by major occupation and major industry, and class of worker; also employment and unemployment, and income and poverty status, by race and Hispanic origin. The same data is given, but with less detail, for counties and places within each congressional district.

I.10. *Census of population and housing. Summary social, economic, and housing characteristics.* Census Bureau. C 3.223/23:990 CPH-5-no. decennial. RRG 1-2.

Separate reports for each state, the District of Columbia, Puerto Rico, the Virgin Islands, and a U.S. summary. This summary series gives employment/unemployment statistics by state, county, and city. Tables on income and poverty status give per capita income by state, county, and city, median income for households, and income below poverty level by age for state, county, and city. This summary is superseded, but with considerably more detail, by the *Social and economic characteristics* (I.12).

I.11.   *Census of population and housing (1990). Summary tape file (STF) 3.* Census Bureau. C 3.282/2:CD 90-3A-D. decennial. RRG 1-2.
Summary tape file (STF)[3] comes in five formats: computer tape reels, computer tape cartridges, microcomputer compact discs (CD-ROM), online (in CENDATA), and microfiche. This entry and documents classification number is for the CD-ROM format, this being the first appearance of a *Summary tape file 3* created in the form of a compact disc. *STF 3* provides data on a wide variety of population and housing topics. It comes in four main versions: A, B, C, and D. *STF 3A* includes employment/unemployment and earnings/income statistics for states, county/metro areas and places (including those under 10,000) by census tracts (see also I.8) and block groups where applicable. The other versions of *STF 3: B, C,* and *D,* give the same tables only the geography is different: *STF 3B* provides data by ZIP codes, *3C* provides summary data by United States, regions, divisions, states, counties, places of 10,000 or more, and MCDs, and *3D* by congressional district. *STF 3B, C,* and *D* will have the same classification stem, only the letter name will change, e.g., C 3.282/2:CD 90-3B (C, D).

I.12.   *Census of population. Social and economic characteristics.* Census Bureau. C 3.223/7:990 CP-2-no. decennial. RRG 1-2.
Series of reports for the United States (summary), each of the 50 states, the District of Columbia, Puerto Rico, and the Virgin Islands of the United States. Gives social and economic data for states, counties, and places of 2,500 or more inhabitants.   Data by place include employment/

unemployment and earnings by sex, race, and Hispanic origin.

I.13. *Census of population. Social and economic characteristics. Metropolitan areas.* Census Bureau. C 3.223/7-3: 990 CP-2-1B/sec.1-6. decennial. RRG 1-2.

This report on metropolitan areas appears separately for the first time in the 1990 census. In the census for 1980, the data appeared in the series *General social and economic characteristics.* Summary social and economic characteristics for the U.S. and metropolitan areas, both inside and outside, are given in section (or volume) 1. Detailed characteristics are given for metropolitan areas in the remaining five volumes.

I.14. *Census of population. Social and economic characteristics. Urbanized areas.* Census Bureau. C 3.223/7-4:990 CP-2-1C/sec.1-6. decennial. RRG 1-2.

This report on urbanized areas appears separately for the first time in the 1990 census. In the census of 1980, the data appeared in the series *General social and economic characteristics.* Provides summary of social and economic characteristics for the U.S., urban and rural, and size of place. Detailed characteristics are given for metropolitan areas in the remaining five volumes.

Irregularly Updated Publications

I.15. *County and city data book. A Statistical abstract supplement: states, counties, cities of 25,000 or more, places of 2,500 or more.* Census Bureau. C 3.134/2:C 83/2/yr. irreg., approximately every five years. RRG 1-2.

Presents a variety of information on states, counties, cities, and smaller places in the United States. Includes statistics on area and population, employment/ unemployment and income/earnings, manufactures, retail and wholesale trade, and service industries.

I.16. *Employment, hours, and earnings, states and areas, 1987-92.* BLS. L 2.3:2411. irreg. RRG 1-2.

Presents monthly and annual average data on employment, hours, and earnings in states and metropolitan areas by major industry for 1987-92. Data are obtained from the Current Employment Survey[2]. Data in this compendium are supplemented on a current basis by the monthly publication *Employment and earnings* (I.1).

I.17.   *Employment, hours, and earnings, United States, 1909-94.* BLS. 2 v. L 2.3:2445/v.1-2. irreg. RRG 1-2.
Presents historical monthly and annual average data on national establishment-based employment, hours, and earnings by detailed industry for the nation's nonagricultural workers. Volume 1 covers goods-producing industries, and volume 2, service-producing industries. Supplemented annually by *Supplement to Employment and earnings* (I.6). Supplemented on a current basis by the monthly publication *Employment and earnings* (I.1). State and local data are available in a companion volume, *Employment, hours, and earnings, states and areas* (I.16).

I.18.   *Employment, hours, and earnings, United States, 1981-93.* BLS. L 2.3:2429. irreg. RRG 1-2.
Presents revised monthly and annual average data on national establishment-based employment, hours, and earnings by detailed industry for the nation's nonagricultural workers. This bulletin, combined with pre-1981 data published in *Employment, hours, and earnings, United States, 1909-94* (I.17), comprises all published historical series of national data derived from the Current Employment Survey.[2] Most of the data are supplemented on a current basis by *Employment and earnings* (I.1).

I.19.   *Handbook of labor statistics.* BLS. L 2.3/5:yr. irreg., approximately every three to five years. RRG 1-2.
Makes available in one volume all of the BLS major statistical series from the earliest reliable data through to the present.   Gives detailed statistics on employment, unemployment, and earnings by population groups. Also

gives labor force statistics by industry and occupation with population breakdowns. Includes statistics on various other topics such as manufacturing, productivity data, collective bargaining, and labor statistics for ten major industrial countries.

I.20. *Labor force statistics derived from the Current Population Survey, 1948-87.* BLS. L 2.3:2307. irreg., approxi-mately every five years. RRG 1-2.

Presents the second comprehensive historical collection of national data on the characteristics of the employed, the unemployed, and persons not in the labor force. Gives median weekly earnings by age, sex, and race, also by detailed industry. Statistics obtained from the Current Population Survey (CPS).[1] Most of the data contained in this compendium are supplemented on a current basis by *Employment and earnings* (I.1) and *Monthly labor review* (I.3).

Sources with Selective Data on Employment/Unemployment and Income Data

Periodicals

I.21. *Economic indicators.* Prepared for the Joint Economic Committee by the Council of Economic Advisers. Y 4.Ec 7:Ec 7/yr./no. monthly. RRG 1-2.

Gives pertinent economic information with statistical tables and graphs on prices, employment/ unemployment, wages, production, business activity, purchasing power, credit, money, and federal finance.

I.22. *Survey of current business.* Commerce Dept., Bureau of Economic Analysis. C 59.11:v./no. monthly. RRG 1-2.

Contains estimates and analyses of U.S. economic activity. Features include section on business cycle indicators with tables for 250 series and charts for 130 series; and a section of current business statistics presenting over 1,900 major economic series (including "Labor force, employment, and earnings") obtained from public and private sources. Supplemented by *Business statistics: a supplement to the Survey of current business* (I.26).

Annuals, Biennials, etc.

I.23.   *Economic report of the President, transmitted to the Congress, together with Annual report of the Council of Economic Advisers.* President of the United States. Pr 4[1].9:yr. (classification number changes with every new president) annual.
Reports the Administration's financial plan for each fiscal year. Also includes appendices "On the activities of the Council of Economic Advisers," and "Statistical tables relating to income, employment, and production." These tables include labor force statistics for seven major industrial countries. *Economic report of the President* also included in the CD-ROM *National economic, social, and environmental data book.(NESE DB).* C 1.88/2:yr./no. quarterly.

I.24.   *Foreign labor trends.* Labor Dept., Bureau of International Affairs. L 29.16:[no.,yr.] annual. RRG 1-2.
With separate reports for each country, these reports prepared by the American Embassy describe and analyze the labor trends in approximately 60 countries a year. They cover significant labor developments, including labor-management relations, trade unions, employment/unemployment, wages and working conditions, labor and government, labor administration, training, labor and politics, labor migration, and international labor activities. A list of key labor indicators is included in most reports. Also submits reports on labor trends common to groups of countries, and on international labor issues. *Foreign labor trends* also included in the CD-ROM *National trade data bank (NTDB)* C 1.88:yr./mo.CD. monthly.

Australia L 29.16:Au 7/2/yr.

Austria L 29.16:Au 7/yr.

Bangladesh L 29.16:B 22/yr.

Belgium L 29.16:B 41/yr.

Bolivia L 29.16:B 63/yr.

Brazil L 29.16:B 73/yr.

Canada L 29.16:C 16/yr.

Chile L 29.16:C 43/yr.

China L 29.16:C 44/yr.

Colombia L 29.16:C 72/yr.

Costa Rica L 29.16:C 84/yr.

Denmark L 29.16:D 41/yr.

Dominican Republic L 29.16:D 71/yr.

Eastern Caribbean L 29.16:C 19

Ecuador L 29.16:Ec 9/yr.

Egypt L 29.16:Egy 9/yr.

El Salvador L 29.16:El 8/yr.

Finland L 29.16:F 49/yr.

France L 29.16:F 84/yr.

Germany K 29.16:G 31/yr.

Ghana L 29.16:G 35/yr.

Greece L 29.16:G 81/yr.

Guyana L 29.16:G 99/yr.

Haiti L 29.16:H 12/yr.

Honduras L 29.16:H 75/yr.

Hong Kong L 29.16:H 75/2/yr.

Iceland L 29.16:Ic 2/yr.

India L 29.16:In 2/2/yr.

Indonesia L 29.16:In 2/yr.

Ireland L 29.16:Ir 2/yr.

Italy L 29.16:It l/yr.

Jamaica L 29.16:J 22/yr.

Japan L 29.16:J 27/yr.

Jordan L 29.16:J 76/yr.

Kenya L 29.16:K 42/yr.

Korea L 29.16:K 84/yr.

Kuwait L 29.16:K 96/yr.

Liberia L 29.16:L 61/yr.

Malaysia L 29.16:M 29/yr.

Mexico L 29.16:M 57/yr.

Morocco L 29.16:M 82/yr.

Netherlands L 29.16:N 38/yr.

New Zealand L 29.16:N 42/yr.

Nicaragua L 29.16:N 51/yr.

Nigeria L 29.16:N 56/yr.

Norway L 29.16:N 83/yr.

Panama L 29.16:P 19/yr.

Peru L 29.16:P 43/yr.

Philippines L 29.16:P 53/yr.

Portugal L 29.16:P 83/yr.

Senegal L 29.16:Se 5/yr.

Singapore L 29.16:Si 6/yr.

South Africa L 29.16:So 8a/yr.

Suriname L 29.16:Su 7/yr.

Sweden L 29.16:Sw 3/yr.

Switzerland L 29.16:Sw 6/yr.

Taiwan L 29.16:T 13/yr.

Thailand L 29.16:T 32/yr.

Trinidad and Tobago L 29.16:T 73/yr.

Tunisia L 29.16:T 83/yr.

Turkey L 29.16:T 84/yr.

United Kingdom L 29.16:Un 3/2/yr.

Uruguay L 29.16:Ur 8/yr.

USSR L 29.16:Un 3/yr.

Yugoslavia L 29.16:Y 9/yr.

Zaire L 29.16:Z 1/yr.

Zimbabwe L 29.16:Z 6/yr.

Foreign labor trends also covers labor developments in groups of countries, and on international labor issues:

Informal sector and workers rights L 29.16:Se 2/yr.

International child labor problems L 29.26:C 43/2/yr.

International trade secretariats: the industrial trade union internationals L 29.16:In 8/yr.

Labor shortages in east Asian countries L 29.16:As 4/yr.

A look at workers rights in Eastern Europe L 29.16:Eu 7/yr.

Privatization in Latin America L 29.16:L 34/yr.

Worker rights in U.S. policy L 29.16:W 89/2/yr.

I.25.   *Population profile of the United States.* Census Bureau. C 3.186/8:yr. annual

Brings together under one cover a wide range of sample survey data on social and economic data for the nation as a whole. Contains sections "Labor force and occupation," "Money, income," and "Poverty." Considerable data are given in graphic form.

I.26.   *Business statistics; a supplement to the Survey of current business.* Commerce Dept., Bureau of Economic Analysis. C 59.11/3:yr. biennial. RRG 1-2.

Presents historical data and methodological notes for approximately 2,100 series that appear in the *Survey of current business* (I.22). The main body of the publication presents annual data for 1961 to the present and monthly data for the last four years for the approximately 1,900 series drawn from public and private sources. This section includes tables "Labor force, employment, and earnings," giving data for the same time periods.

I.27.   *State and metropolitan area data book. A Statistical abstract supplement.* Census Bureau. C 3.134/5:yr. irreg., approximately every five years. RRG 1-2.

Presents a variety of information on states, metropolitan areas, and central cities of the United States. Employment/unemployment and income are among the many subjects covered.

Chapter Two

Sources on
Employment/Unemployment
(not including income)

Periodicals

II.1.   *Commerce   publications   update.* Commerce   Dept.
         C 1.24/3:v./no. biweekly.
         Listing of the latest publications and press releases on
         business, the economy, trade, scientific and technical
         developments, and related topics from the U.S. Dept. of
         Commerce. Each issue contains the table "Key economic
         indicators," covering 23 economic areas including employ-
         ment and unemployment for quarter or month ending one to
         three months prior to date of issue. Issued biweekly, the
         statistics provided here are particularly useful for their
         timeliness.

II.2.   *Employment-unemployment: Hearings before the Joint
         Economic Committee, Congress of the United States.* Joint
         Economic Committee. Y 4.Ec 7:Em 7/12/pt./no. monthly.
         Monthly hearings with testimony focusing on the
         employment/unemployment situation and the statistics the
         BLS has compiled on this issue. Statistical data are mainly
         reprints from *Monthly labor review* (I.3) and *Employment
         situation* (I.2). May also contain reprints of data from other

publications of the BLS and from various publications of the Census Bureau.

II.3.   *Federal Reserve bulletin.* Board of Governors of the Federal Reserve System. FR 1.3:v./no. monthly.

Divided into two parts, part 1 reports on the activities of the federal banking system and major developments related to economics and finance. Part 2 covers "Financial and business statistics" in tabular form, including a table "Labor force, employment, and unemployment."

II.4.   *News. State and metropolitan area employment and unemployment.* BLS. L 2.111/5:(date) monthly.

Presents labor force employment and unemployment data for states and selected metropolitan areas from the Current Population Survey[1] (household survey), the Current Employment Survey[2] (establishment survey), and the Local Area Unemployment Statistics[4] program. Employment by state is cross indexed by major industry.

II.5.   *Unemployment in states and local areas.* BLS. L 2.41/9: (date) monthly, with supplement issued irregularly. RRG 1.

Provides provisional, monthly estimates of the labor force employment and unemployment for states, metropolitan areas, counties, and cities of 50,000 or more. These estimates are used for economic analysis and administration of various federal economic assistance programs. Previously published under the title *Employment and unemployment in states and local areas.*

Annuals and Irregular Publications

II.6.   *Geographic profile of employment and unemployment.* BLS. L 2.3/12:yr. annual. RRG 1.

Presents annual averages on employment and unemployment from the Current Population Survey (CPS)[1] covering census regions, states, 50 large metropolitan areas, and 17 cities.

II.7.   *Revised seasonally adjusted labor force statistics, 1978-87.* BLS. L 2.3:2306. irreg., approximately every five years.

RRG 1.

This bulletin presents revised seasonally adjusted data from 1978 through 1987 on the characteristics of the employed, the unemployed, and persons not in the labor force obtained from the Current Population Survey (CPS).[1] The data contained in this bulletin are supplemented on a more current basis by *Employment and earnings* (I.1) and *Monthly labor review* (I.3).

Foreign Countries

II.8.   *Country reports on economic policy and trade practices. Report submitted to the Committee on Foreign Relations, Committee on Finance of the U.S. Senate by the Department of State...* Senate Committee on Foreign Relations. Y 4.F 76/2:S.prt.no. annual.

Intended primarily as a general guide to the economic conditions of a specific country (approximately 90 countries) and to provide a single, comprehensive and comparative analysis of the economic policies and trade practices of these countries with which the U.S. has an economic or trade relationship. A "Key economic indicators" is provided for each country and covers "Income, production and employment," "Money and prices," and "Balance of payments and trade." "Income, production and employment" includes number in labor force and percent unemployment.

II.9.   *Foreign economic trends and their implications for the United States.* International Trade Administration. C 61.11:[no.,yr.]

Series of semiannual and annual reports giving a brief report on the economy of each country and its implications for the U.S. trade and investment. Each issue has a "Key economic indicators" table which includes employment/unemployment. Gives summary reports on key elements of the economy such as foreign trade, monetary situation, living costs, production, and labor market situation. Reports prepared by foreign officers and data derived from foreign officers and data derived from foreign government sources. Frequency is given for semiannuals only; the others are annual. For more detailed information on employment and earnings in foreign countries, see *Foreign labor trends* (I.24). *Foreign economic trends* was discontinued in 1993. Similar data continue to be covered in a new series *Country commercial guides* which is included in the CD-ROM *National trade data bank (NTDB)*. C 1.88:yr./no./CD. monthly.

Algeria C 61.11:Al 3/yr.

Argentina C 61.11:Ar 3/yr.

Aruba C 61.11:Ar 8/yr.

Australia C 61.11:Au 7/yr.

Austria C 61.11:Au 7/2/yr.

Bahamas C 61.11:B 14/yr.

Bahrain C 61.11:B 14/2/yr.

Bangladesh C 61.11:B 22/yr.

Barbados C 61.11:B 23/yr.

Belgium C 61.11:B 41/yr. semiannual.

Belize C 61.11:B 41/2/yr.

Benin C 61.11:B 43/yr.

Bolivia C 61.11:B 63/yr.

Botswana C 61.11:B 65/yr.

Brazil C 61.11:B 73/yr.

Bulgaria C 61.11:B 87/yr.

Burkina Faso C 61.11:B 91/yr.

Burma C 61.11:B 92/yr.

Burundi C 61.11:B 95/yr.

Cameroon C 61.11:C 14/yr.

Canada C 61.11:C 16/yr. semiannual.

Cape Verde C 61.11:C 17/yr.

Central African Republic C 61.11:C 33/yr.

Chad C 61.11:C 34/yr.

Chile C 61.11:C 43/yr. semiannual.

China (People's Republic of) C 61.11:C 44/yr.

Colombia C 61.11:C 71/yr.

Congo C 61.11:C 76/yr.

Costa Rica C 61.11:C 82/2/yr.

Cyprus C 61.11:C 99/yr.

Czechoslovakia. C 61.11:C 99/2/yr.

Ecuador. C 61.11:Ec 9/yr. semiannual.

Egypt C 61.11:Eg 9/yr.

El Salvador C 61.11:Sa 3/yr.

Equatorial Guinea C 61.11:Eq 2/yr.

Ethiopia C 61.11:Et 3/yr.

Fiji C 61.11:F 47/yr.

Finland C 61.11:F 49/yr.

France C 61.11:F 84/yr. semiannual.

Gabon C 61.11:G 11/yr.

Germany C 61.11:G 31/yr.

Ghana C 61.11:G 34/yr.

Greece C 61.11:G 81/yr.

Grenada C 61.11:G 86/yr.

Guatemala C 61.11:G 93/yr.

Guinea C 61.11:G 94/yr.

Guyana C 61.11:G 99/yr.

Haiti C 61.11:H 12/yr.

Honduras C 61.11:H 75/2/yr.

Hong Kong C 61.11:H 75/yr.

Hungary C 61.11:H 89/yr.

Iceland C 61.11:Ic 2/yr.

India C 61.11:In 2/2/yr.

Indonesia C 61.11:In 2/yr. semiannual.

Ireland C 61.11:Ir 2/yr.

Israel C 61.11:Is 7/yr.

Italy C 61.11:It 1/yr.   semiannual.

Ivory Coast C 61.11:C 82/yr.

Jamaica C 61.11:J 22/yr.

Japan C 61.11:J 27/yr.   semiannual.

Jordan C 61.11:J 76/yr.

Kenya C 61.11:K 42/yr.

Korea C 61.11:K 84/yr.

Kuwait C 61.11:K 96/yr.

Laos C 61.11:L 29/2/yr.

Lesotho C 61.11:L 56/yr.

Liberia C 61.11:L 61/yr.

Luxembourg C 61.11:L 97/yr.

Madagascar C 61.11:M 26/yr.

Malawi C 61.11:M 29/2/yr.

Malaysia C 61.11:M 29/yr.

Mali C 61.11:M 29/3/yr.

Mauritania C 61.11:M 44/2/yr.

Mauritius C 61.11:M 44/yr.

Mexico C 61.11:M 57/yr.

Morocco C 61.11:M 82/yr.

Mozambique C 61.11:M 87/yr.

Namibia C 61.11:N 15/yr.

Nepal C 61.11:N 35/yr.

Netherlands C 61.11:N 38/yr.

Netherlands Antilles C 61.11:N 38/2/yr.

New Zealand C 61.11:N 42Z/yr.

Niger C 61.11:N 56/2/yr.

Nigeria C 61.11:N 56/yr.

Norway C 61.11:N 83/yr.

Oman C 61.11:Om 1/yr.

Pakistan C 61.11:P 17/yr.

Panama C 61.11:P 19/yr.

Papua-New Guinea C 61.11:P 19/2/yr.

Paraguay C 61.11:P 21/yr.

Peru C 61.11:P 43/yr.

Philippines C 61.11:P 53/yr.   semiannual.

Poland C 61.11:P 75/yr.

Portugal C 61.11:P 83/yr.

Qatar C 61.11:Q 1/yr.

Romania C 61.11:R 66/yr.

Rwanda C 61.11:R 94/yr.

Saudi Arabia C 61.11:Sa 8/yr.

Senegal C 61.11:Se 5/yr.

Sierra Leone C 61.11:Si 1/yr.

Singapore C 61.11:Si 6/yr.

Somalia C 61.11:So 5/yr.

South Africa C 61.11:So 8a/yr.

Spain C 61.11:Sp 1/yr.   semiannual.

Sri Lanka C 61.11:Sr 3/yr.

St. Lucia C 61.11:Sa 2L/yr.

St. Vincent and Grenadines C 61.11:Sa 2v/yr.

Sudan C 61.11:Su 2/yr.

Suriname C 61.11:Su 7/yr.

Swaziland C 61.11:Sw 2/yr.

Sweden C 61.11:Sw 3/yr.

Switzerland C 61.11:Sw 6/yr.   semiannual.

Syria C 61.11:Sy 8/yr.

Taiwan C 61.11:T 13/yr.   semiannual.

Tanzania C 61.11:T 15/yr.

Thailand C 61.11:T 32/yr.   semiannual.

Togo C 61.11:T 57/yr.

Trinidad and Tobago C 61.11:T 73/yr.

Tunisia C 61.11:T 83/yr.

Turkey C 61.11:T 84/yr.

Uganda C 61.11:Ug 1/yr.

United Arab Emirates C 61.11:Un 3/yr.

United Kingdom C 61.11:K 59/yr.   semiannual.

Uruguay C 61.11:Ur 8/yr.

Venezuela C 61.11:V 55/yr.   semiannual.

Yemen Arab Republic C 61.11:Y 3/yr.

Zaire C 61.11:Z 1/yr.

Zambia C 61.11:Z 1/2/yr.

Zimbabwe C 61.11:Z 6/yr.

II.10.   *Handbook of economic statistics.* Central Intelligence Agency. PrEx 3.10/7-5:yr. annual.

Provides statistics for all Communist countries and selected non-Communist countries (the Big Seven: U.S., Canada, Japan, France, Italy, the U.K., and Germany), and selective statistics of other countries, e.g., EC, OECD, OPEC, and less developed countries. Gives statistics on agricultural and non-agricultrual labor force, and industrial employment (manufacturing, mining, and construction) for the past 25 years for all Communist countries and the Big Seven. Also gives percent of unemployment for the Big Seven for the past 25 years. *Handbook of economic statistics* also included in the CD-ROM *National trade data bank (NTDB).* C 1.88:yr./ mo./CD. monthly.

II.11.   *The world factbook.* Central Intelligence Agency. PrEx 3.10/7-2:yr. annual.

Prepared in cooperation with other government agencies, provides brief information on the geography, people, government, economy, communications, and defense of over 200 countries. Economy section includes percent of unemployment. *World factbook* also included in the CD-ROM *National trade data bank (NTDB).* C 1.88:yr./ mo./CD.

Chapter Three

Employment Projections

III.1. *Occupational outlook quarterly.* BLS. L 2.70/4:v.no. quarterly.

Provides current information on employment trends and outlook, supplementing and bringing up to date information in *Occupational outlook handbook* (III.4). Every two years includes "Job outlook in brief", summarizing employment projections up to 10 to 15 years for 250 occupations.

III.2. *Career guide to industries.* BLS. L 2.3/4-3:yr. annual.

A companion publication to *Occupational outlook handbook* (III.4), the guide provides information on careers from an industrial perspective. Arranged by industry, gives current year of employment for each industry with projections of 15 years. Current average earnings are provided for selected occupations for most industries.

III.3. *The American workforce: 1992-2005.* BLS. L 2.3:2452. biennial.

Each issue includes articles reprinted from *Monthly labor review* (I.3) on economic and employment projections for approximately the next 15 years. Statistical tables cover current employment and projections to 2005 by major and detailed industry and by major and detailed occupation. Appendix includes tables on population, labor force, and labor force participation by age, sex, race, and Hispanic origin for 1992 with projections for 1995 through 2005. Description based on 1994 edition. Previously published under the titles: *Outlook 1990-2005* (1992); *Outlook 2000* (1990); *Projections 2000* (1988).

III.4.   *Occupational outlook handbook*. BLS. L 2.3/4:yr. biennial. RRG 1-2.

Provides detailed information on about 225 occupations. Occupations that require lengthy education or training are given the most attention. Includes employment statistics, salaries, and job outlook for each occupation. Supplemented by *Occupational outlook quarterly* (III.1) and *Occupational projections and training data* (III.5). *Occupational outlook handbook* also available on CD-ROM. L 2.3/4-4:yr./CD

III.5.   *Occupational projections and training data, a statistical and research supplement to Occupational outlook handbook*. BLS. L 2.3/4-2:yr. biennial.

Provides statistics and technical data underlying the qualitative information presented in *Occupational outlook handbook* (III.4). Occupational employment projections usually cover 10 to 15 years. Gives current percentage of employees in occupations by age, sex, and race.

III.6.   *BEA regional projections to 2040*. Commerce Dept., Bureau of Economic Analysis. C 59.17:yr./v.1-3. 3 v. quinquennial.

Presents projections to 2040 of economic activity and population for the nation and the states, metropolitan statistical areas, and BEA economic areas. Vol. 1: *States*, presents projections for the nation and the states. Provides projections for population in three age groups, personal income, and employment and earnings, each of which is presented for 57 industrial groups. Shows projections for 1995 through 2040 and gives historical data for 1973 through 1988. Vol. 2: *Metropolitan statistical areas*, presents projections for metropolitan areas for employment by industry and earnings for 1995 through 2040. Vol. 3: *BEA economic areas*, presents projections of economic activity and population projections for Bureau of Economic Analysis economic areas and the nation.

Chapter Four

Employment/Unemployment—
Separate Reports on Minorities, Ancestry
Groups, Women, and Special Population
Groups

Minorities (General)

IV.1.   *Employment in perspective: minority workers.* BLS.
L 2.41/11-2:nos. quarterly.
Covers employment status of African-Americans and Hispanic Americans by detailed origin.

IV.2.   *Job patterns for minorities and women in private industry.*
EEOC. Y 3.Eq 2:12-7/yr. annual. RRG 1.
Presents employment statistics on race (including white population), ethnic group, and sex for each of nine occupational groups: craft workers, operatives, laborers, service workers, officials and managers, professionals, technicians, sales, office and clerical. Covers U.S., states, and PMSAs. Compiled from data reported to EEOC under Title 7 of the Civil Rights Act of 1964. Convenient for comparing minority labor statistics with that of the white population. This is the only document that regularly updates labor force statistics for all minority and ethnic groups.

IV.3.   *Reports to the Congress required by the Fair labor standards act.* BLS, Employment Standards Administration.

L 36.9:yr. annual.

Contains two reports: 1. "Minimum wage and maximum hours under the *Fair labor standards act*, annual report." 2. "Groups with historically high incidences of unemployment, biennial report." Gives statistics on unemployment of selected groups: youth, minorities, older workers, and Vietnam-era veterans.

IV.4.   *Census of population and housing. Equal employment opportunity file* [on CD-ROM]. Census Bureau. C 3.283: CD 90-EEO-1. decennial.

Covers employment by detailed occupation, by sex, race, and Hispanic origin for U.S., states, counties, and places of 50,000 or more. Convenient reference for comparing occupational employment of the white population with that of other races.

African-Americans

IV.5.   *Black news digest: news from the United States Dept. of Labor, Office of Information and Public Affairs.* The Office. L 1.20/6:date. weekly.

This newsletter contains articles and statistics on blacks in the labor force as well as on the labor force in general. The monthly "Employment situation," gives employment/ unemployment by age and race (white, black).

IV.6.   *The black population in the United States. Current population reports. Population characteristics series P-20.* Census Bureau. C 3.186:P 20/no. annual.

Presents statistical portrait of the demographic, social, and economic status of blacks based on the Current Population Survey (CPS).[1] Gives tables on employment, unemployment, and income by sex and race (white, black).

IV.6A. *Census of population. [Population subject reports]. Characteristics of the black population.* Census Bureau. C 3.223/10:990 CP-3-6. decennial.

Data in these detailed and comprehensive subject reports on

the black population are taken from the decennial census of population. They cover population, social, labor force, economic, and housing characteristics for black Americans. Labor force characteristics include employment/unemployment, and employment by industry, occupation, and class of worker.

IV.7. *We the American... blacks.* Census Bureau. C 3.2:Am 3/14. decennial.

Concise information booklets on black Americans with data provided by the decennial census of population and housing. Includes population, social, and economic data. Economic areas cover employment/unemployment, occupation, income, and poverty rates. Most of the data is given in graphic form.

Asian and Pacific Islander Americans

IV.8. *Census of population. [Population subject reports]. Asians and Pacific Islanders in the United States.* Census Bureau. C 3.223/10:990 CP-3-5. decennial.

Data in these detailed and comprehensive subject reports on Asian and Pacific Islanders are taken from the decennial census of population. They cover population, social, labor force, economic, and housing characteristics for all Asians, and for specific Asian and Pacific Islander groups, e.g., Chinese, Filipino, Japanese, etc. Labor force characteristics cover employment/unemployment, and employment by industry, occupation, and class of worker. This subject report is also available on CD-ROM under the title: *Characteristics of the Asian and Pacific Islander population in the United States.* Subject summary tape file (SSTF) 5. C 3.286:CD 90 SSTF 05.

IV.9. *We the American... Asians.* Census Bureau. C 3.2:Am 3/13. decennial.

Concise information booklets on Asian-Americans with data provided by the decennial census of population and housing. Includes population, social, and economic data. Tables on economic characteristics include employment/unemployment, occupation, income and poverty level. Provides statistics for all Asians as well as for specific Asian origin groups, e.g., Chinese, Filipino, Japanese, etc.

IV.10. *We the American...Pacific Islanders.* Census Bureau. C 3.2:Am 3/15. decennial.

Concise information booklets on Pacific Islander Americans with data provided by the decennial census of population and housing. Tables on selected social and economic characteristics include employment/ unemployment, occupation, income, and poverty level. Provides data for all Pacific Islander Americans as well as for Pacific Islander origin groups, e.g., Hawaiian, Samoan, Tongan, etc.

IV.11. *Asian and Pacific Islander population in the United States. Current population reports. Population characteristics series P 20.* Census Bureau. C 3. 186:P 20/459. irreg.

Issued in 1992, this presents the first Current Population Survey (CPS)[1] report on the demographic, social, and economic characteristics of the Asian and Pacific Islander population in the United States. Includes employment/ unemployment and earnings statistics for the total population, Asian and Pacific Islander population, and white population for the U.S. and the West. Also includes tables on these groups by occupational employment and years of school completed. Informa-tion in this report is based on data from the March 1991 and 1990 supplements to the CPS.[1]

Hispanic Americans

IV.12. *Noticias de la semana: a news summary for Hispanics.* Labor Dept., Office of Information, Publications and Reports. L 1.20/7:date. weekly.

Contains articles of interest for Hispanics and also for the population as a whole on the current labor situation. Gives monthly employment statistics by age, sex, race, and Hispanic origin, and by major occupation and industry.

IV.13. *The Hispanic population in the United States. Current population reports. Population characteristics series P-20.* Census Bureau. C 3.186/14-2:yr. annual.
Presents data on the demographic, social, and economic characteristics of the Hispanic population and its sub groups: Mexican, Puerto Rican, Cuban, Central and South American, and other Spanish origins. Includes detailed tables on employment/unemployment and income.

IV.14. *Census of population. [Population subject reports]. Persons of Hispanic origin in the United States.* Census Bureau. C 3.223/10:990 CP-3-3. decennial.
Data in these detailed and comprehensive subject reports on Hispanics are taken from the decennial census of population. They cover population, social, labor force, economic, and housing characteristics for all Hispanics and for specific Hispanic origin groups, e.g., Chilean, El Salvadoran, Mexican, etc. Labor force characteristics cover employment/unemployment, and employment by occupation, industry, and class of worker. *Persons of Hispanic origin in the United States* also available on CD-ROM. C 3.286:CD 90 SSTF 03.

IV.14A. *We the American...Hispanics.* Census Bureau.   C 3.2: Am 3/18. decennial.
Concise information booklets on Hispanic Americans with data provided by the decennial census of population and housing. Tables cover social and economic characteristics which include percentage employment figures of Hispanics by major occupation with comparison to the non-Hispanic population.

Indians of North America

IV.14B. *Census of population. [Population subject reports]. Characteristics of American Indians by tribe and language.* Census Bureau. C 3.223/10:990 CP-3-7/sec.1-2. decennial.
Data in these detailed and comprehensive subject reports on American Indians are taken from the decennial census of

population. They cover population, social, labor force, economic, and housing characteristics by American Indian tribes. Included in these reports are work status, employment by major industry, and occupation for the U.S., states, and metropolitan areas.

IV.15.   *Census of population. Social and economic characteristics. American Indian and Alaska native areas.* Census Bureau. C 3.223/7-2:990 CP-2-1A/sec.1-2. decennial.

This report on American Indian and Alaskan native areas appears separately for the first time in the 1990 census. In 1980 the data appeared in the series *General social and economic characteristics.* Covers detailed social and economic characteristics of American Indian, Eskimo, or Aleut persons. Tables provide data for individual American Indian reservations and trust lands, and Alaska native village areas, with county and state parts of each individual area. Includes employment/unemployment and occupation by sex.

IV.16.   *We the... first Americans.* Census Bureau. C 3.2:Am 3/19/yr. decennial.

Concise information booklets on American Indians and Alaska natives with data provided by the decennial census of population and housing. Includes labor force participation rate, employment rate by major occupation, median family income, and poverty rate. Data are given for American Indians, Eskimos, and Aleuts. Most of the information is given in graphic form.

Ancestry and the Foreign Born

IV.17.   *Census of population. [Population subject reports]. Ancestry of the population in the United States.* Census Bureau. C 3.223/10:990 CP-3-2. decennial.

Data in these detailed and comprehensive subject reports are from the decennial census of population. Provides population, housing, social,. economic, and labor force characteristics on the ancestry and on the foreign born of the U.S. population. Labor force data include employment/unemployment,

employment by major occupation and major industry, and by class of worker. All tables provide data on ancestry groups, and on the foreign born by nativity, citizenship, and year of entry. *Ancestry of the population in the United States* also available on CD-ROM. C 3.286:CD 90 SSTF 02.

IV.18. *Census of population. [Population subject reports]. The foreign-born population in the United States.* Census Bureau. C 3.223/10:990 CP-3-1. decennial.

Data in these detailed and comprehensive reports on the foreign-born population in the United States are taken from the decennial census of population. They include general population and housing characteristics, social and labor force characteristics, and income and poverty status of the foreign born. All tables are cross indexed by nativity, citizenship, and year of entry. This subject report on the foreign born is issued for the first time by the census of population, 1990. *The foreign-born population in the United States* also available on CD ROM. C 3.286:CD 90 SSTF 01.

IV.19. *We the American...foreign born.* Census Bureau. C 3.2: Am 3/21/yr. decennial.

Concise information booklets on America's foreign born with data provided by the decennial census of population and housing. Gives labor force data on total foreign born and more detailed data on immigrants from the 11 countries that provide the highest number of foreign born. Data on immigrants from these countries include employment/ unemployment by major occupation, and income and poverty level. Most of the information is given in graphic form.

Women

IV.20. *Women & work: news from the U.S. Dept. of Labor, Office of Information, Publications and Reports.* The Office. L 1.20/8:(date) monthly.

Covers articles on women and the population as a whole on the current labor situation. Periodically gives monthly employment statistics by age, sex, race, and Hispanic origin.

IV.21.   *Employment in perspective: women in the labor force.* BLS.
L 2.41/11:(date) quarterly.
Presents data from the Current Population Survey[1] on
the status of women in the labor force. Gives
employment/unemployment, and unemployment rate of
women, by age and often by race.

IV.22.   *We the American... women.* Census Bureau.   C 3.2:Am
3/6/yr. decennial.
Concise information booklets on American women with data
provided by the decennial census of population and housing.
Includes labor force participation rates by race and Hispanic
origin, median family income with female householder,
poverty rates of persons by age, and sex. Most of the
information is given in graphic form.

IV.23.   *Facts on working women.* Labor Dept., Women's Bureau.
L 36.114/3:yr./no. irreg., several issues per year.
A series of pamphlets, each one dealing with a specific aspect
of women in the labor force. Statistical tables are included in
most pamphlets. Some examples of recent titles: *Earnings
differences between women and men; Black women in the
labor force; Women workers outlook to 2005.*

IV.24.   *Working women: a chartbook.* BLS. L 2.3:2385. irreg.
Chartbook on women in the labor force giving comparisons to
men from 1960 to 1990. Gives employment of women by
occupation and major industry; employment and
unemployment and earnings by age, race, and Hispanic
origin; and labor force participation in nine OECD countries.
Description based on 1991 edition.

Separate Reports on Special Population Groups

Aged

IV.25.   *Census of population and housing. Special tabulation on
aging.* Census Bureau. C 3.281/2:CD 90-AOA1. decennial.
This CD-ROM product released for the first time by

the 1990 census of population and housing gives employment/unemployment and income and poverty status of persons by age from 45-85, and of families, by state, county, metropolitan area, city, and places of 2,500 or more.

IV.26. *Aging America, trends and projections*. Prepared by the U.S. Senate Special Committee on Aging, the American Association of Retired Persons, the Federal Council on the Aging, and the U.S. Administration on Aging. Y 3.F 31/15:2 Ag 4/2/yr. irreg.

Analyzes demographic and socioeconomic trends on the aged population (65 and over) in the U.S., including a section on the aged in selected foreign countries. Gives current and retrospective data on income and labor force participation and gives projections to 2000 of labor force participation for this special segment of the population. Description based on 1991 edition.

Disabled

IV.27. *Chartbook on work disability in the United States*. Dept. of Education, National Institute on Disability and Rehabilitation Research. ED 1.2:D 63/8/yr. irreg.

A reference book on work disability in the U.S. population. Section 4, "Work disability and the labor force," provides employment/unemployment statistics on population with a work disability by state, also by race and Hispanic origin, and employment tables by major occupation and major industry, cross indexed by sex.

IV.28. *Labor force status and other characteristics of persons with a work disability: 1981-88. Current population reports. Special studies. Series P 23, no.160.* Census Bureau. C 3.186:P 23/160. irreg.

Provides data on characteristics of persons with a work disability including employment/unemploy-ment by age, sex, race, and Hispanic origin. Also provides data for this group on employment in major industry and major occupation by sex, race, and Hispanic origin. Comparative statistics are given for two groups: those with a severe disability and those with a disability that is not severe. Comparative statistics are also given for the population without a work disability.

Immigrants

IV.29. *President's comprehensive triennial report on immigration.* Immigration and Naturalization Service. J 21.21:yr. triennial. Mandated by the Immigration Reform and Control Act of 1986, includes number and classification of aliens admitted; estimates of the number of aliens who entered illegally, and a description of the impact of these entries on the economic and social systems of the country; tables on foreign-origin workers in the labor force; percent of employed native and foreign born by industry and occupation; and occupation of employed foreign born by major industry, subdivided by region. Other tables on the labor force give comparisons of native and foreign-born workers. Also tables on aid to noncitizens by the various social assistance service programs, e.g., AFDC, food stamp program, and SSI program.

Refugees

IV.30. *Refugee Resettlement Program; report to the Congress.* Social Security Administration, Family Support Administration. annual. This document is not printed by the Government Printing Office. For location see *American statistics index*, fiche no. 4694-5.
Report on refugee resettlement program activities and funding. Includes tables on refugee employment and unemployment status.

Students

IV.31. *School enrollment—social and economic characteristics of students.* Census Bureau. C 3.186/12:yr. annual.
Presents detailed tabulations of data on school enrollment of the civilian noninstitutional population. Data are from the school enrollment supplement to the Current Population

Survey (CPS).[1] Gives employment status of high school and college students, for vocational education students, and for recent high-school graduates, by age, sex, race, and Hispanic origin.

Trade Union Workers

IV.32   *News. Union members.* BLS. L 2.120/2-12:yr. annual.
Press release covering number of employed union and nonunion workers, by age, sex, race and Hispanic origin, and by major occupation and industry.

Unemployment Insurance Recipients

IV.33.   *Unemployment insurance weekly claims reports.* Dept. of Labor, Employment and Training Administration. L 37.12/2-2:yr./no. weekly.
Provides two tables on unemployment insurance: number of initial claims, and total number claiming benefits for current week and year, with comparisons to previous week and year. Covers the following programs: State Unemployment Insurance, Federal Employees, Newly Discharged Veterans, Railroad Retirement Board, and Extended Benefits. Surveys unemployment insurance activity in the various states with the highest insured unemployment rates and those with the highest initial claims.

Youth

IV.34.   *Youth indicators: trends in the well-being of American youth.* Education Dept., Office of Education Research and Improvement. ED 1.327:yr. irreg.
Compilation of largely statistical data on the youth population through age 24. Includes chapter on youth employment and unemployment. Gives employment of students, high-school graduates, and dropouts. Description based on 1991 edition.

Chapter Five

Employment by Industry/Occupation

Public Sector (Government)

Federal Government

V.1.   *Employment and trends as of... Federal civilian workforce
statistics.* OPM. PM 1.15:nos. bimonthly.
Presents employment information on the federal civilian
workforce based on reports received from each department
and agency in the federal government. Employment statistics
are given by branch, agency, and area (U.S., Washington,
D.C., MSA, and overseas).

V.2.   *Annual report on the employment of minorities, women, and
people with disabilities in the federal government.* EEOC.
Y 3.Eq 2:12-5/yr. annual.
Gives employment percentages for total federal government
and for federal agencies by sex, race, and Hispanic origin.
Also gives these statistics by major occupation for total
government agencies. Similar tables are given for
handicapped employees.

V.3.   *Affirmative employment statistics. Federal civilian
workforce statistics.* OPM. PM 1.10/2-3:yr. biennial.
Provides data on worldwide federal civilian employment
under the Federal Equal Opportunity Recruitment Program.
Employment tables provide data by race and Hispanic origin,
by handicapped status, and by veteran status.

V.4.   *Biennial report of employment by geographic area. Federal
civilian workforce statistics.* OPM. PM 1.10/3:yr. biennial.

Presents civilian employment of the federal government by states, counties, MSAs, foreign countries, and U.S. territories. For states, counties, and MSAs, employment figures are given for selected federal agencies.

V.5.   *Occupations of federal white-collar and blue-collar workers. Federal civilian workforce statistics.* OPM. PM 1.10/2-2:yr. biennial.

Provides data on federal full-time civilian white- and blue-collar workers. Tables are given by occupation, grade or salary range, agency, pay system, sex, and major geographic area (U.S., Washington, D.C., MSA, and overseas). Employment summaries are given for white-collar employment and blue-collar employment. Employees of certain governmental units (U.S.P.S., Congress, CIA, etc.) are not included in this report.

Federal Government—Defense

V.6.   *Military manpower statistics.* Department of Defense. D 1.61:yr./no. quarterly.

Generated from a computerized data base of manpower information, consists of 28 statistical tables providing a variety of information on various aspects of DOD military power. In addition to summary data, detailed data are provided by military or defense component, type of personnel (officer, enlisted) and location around the world. Selected tables also provide data on women in the military.

V.7.   *Defense almanac.* American Forces Information Service. D 2.15/3:yr. annual.

A special annual issue of the bimonthly report, *Defense*, this overview of DOD operations covers mainly organization, budget, and personnel. Gives detailed breakdown of Armed Services personnel—number of officers and enlisted personnel by rank and branch of service, minorities and women by rank and service branch. Also statistics on civilian personnel and military retirees. The bimonthly report contains little statistical data and therefore is not included in this bibliography.

V.8.   *Department of Defense selected manpower statistics.* Dept. of Defense. D 1.61/4:yr. annual.
Provides basic manpower data including active duty, civilian, retired, and reserve military personnel of the Dept. of Defense. Each section has a short narrative with a general description of the contents and selected highlights, displaying increases/decreases from a prior fiscal year, and general trends. Includes historical tables on active duty personnel from 1789 through the present.

V.9.   *Projected defense purchases: detail by industry and state.* Office of the Secretary of Defense. D 1.57/11-2:yr.-yr. biennial.
Presents six-year estimates of the following: defense purchases from 50 SIC industries that are major defense suppliers; defense-related employment, by occupational category; and defense and defense-related spending that may occur in each of the 50 states and the District of Columbia. Description based on the edition covering the projections for 1991-1997.

Federal Government—Postal Service

V.10.   *Annual report of the Postmaster General.* U.S. Postal Service. P 1.1:yr. annual.
Covers postal operations, rates, finances, mail volume, and employment. Gives the number of employees for the last five years by occupation (postmaster, clerks, delivery carriers, etc.).

State, County, and Local Government

V.11.   *City employment. Government employment;GE;yr-no.2.* Census Bureau. C 3.140/2-3:yr. annual.
Provides statistics on municipal government employment, average earnings of employees, and payrolls for individual

cities with a population of 50,000 or more by governmental function for the month of October each year.

V.12.   *County government employment. Government employment;GE;yr-no.4.* Census Bureau. C 3.140/2-5:yr. annual. Provides statistics on county government employment, average earnings of employees, and payroll, with breakdown by governmental function, for the month of October each year.

V.13.   *Job patterns for minorities and women in state and local government.* EEOC. Y 3.Eq 2:12-4-yr. annual. Chiefly statistical tables on employment and salaries in state and local government by age, sex, race, and Hispanic origin. Tables cover national, state, and local summaries, with separate summaries for each state. Also summaries by major job categories and governmental function.

V.14.   *Public employment. Government employment:GE;yr-no.1.* Census Bureau. C 3.140/2-4:yr. annual. Provides state-by-state statistics, with comparisons to local government, on employment and payrolls, and average earnings by governmental function. Also provides comparative statistics on employment of federal, state and local governments.

V.15.   *Census of governments.* Census Bureau. C 3.145/4:yr/ v.3/no.1-2. quinquennial. A four-volume set with multiple parts to each volume covering four major subject fields: government organization, taxable property values, public employment, and government finances. Vol. 3, *Public employment*, covers employment and earnings, and will therefore be the only one considered here. Vol. 3, no. 1, covers employment and average earnings of employees of major local governments. Vol. 3, no. 2, covers employment and average earnings of employees of state and local governments by function.

Private sector—General Sources

Periodicals

V.16   *News. Employment and wages in foreign-owned businesses in the United States.* BLS. L 2.41/12:yr.no. quarterly.
This news release gives average monthly employment and wages of foreign-owned U.S. establishments and all U.S. establishments by 50 four-digit SIC industries. Also employment and wages by state and major industry division. Additional tables cover employment and wages of foreign-owned U.S. establishments in selected counties, and employment and wages by major industry and country of ultimate beneficial owner.

V.17.   *Occupational outlook quarterly.* BLS. L 2.70/4:v.no. quarterly.
Provides current information on employment trends and outlook, supplementing and bringing up to date information in *Occupational outlook handbook* (V.24). Every two years includes "Job outlook in brief" summarizing employment projections up to 10 to 15 years for 250 occupations.

V.18.   *Trade and employment.* Census Bureau. C 3.269:TM-(date). quarterly.
A joint effort of the Bureau of the Census and the Bureau of Labor Statistics. Combines the employment data provided by the BLS with the export and import data produced by the Census Bureau. Gives employment of nonagricultural establishments for exports and imports by industry and commodity.

Annuals

V.19.   *Career guide to industries.* BLS. L 2.3/4-3:yr. annual.
A companion publication to *Occupational outlook handbook* (V.24), the guide provides information on careers from an industrial perspective. Arranged by industry, gives current year of employment for each industry with projections of 15 years. Current average earnings are provided for selected occupations for most industries.

V.20.   *County business patterns.* Census Bureau. C 3.204/3:nos./ yr. annual.
Series of 53 reports on business establishments, employment and payroll, one for each state, District of Columbia, Puerto Rico, and a U.S. summary. By SIC 2-4 digit industry, gives data on establishments, employment, payroll, and establishments by employment size. State reports give data for state and counties. U.S. summary gives the same data at the national level. Also includes tables on employment, payroll, and establishments by employment size for states and counties. *County business patterns* also available on CD-ROM. C 3.204/4:yr./CD.

V.21.   *Foreign direct investment in the United States. Operations of U.S. affiliates of foreign companies.* Commerce Dept., Economics and Statistics Administration, Bureau of Economic Analysis. C 59.20:yr. annual.
Issued in two parts, one giving revised figures for a given year, the other preliminary figures for the following year. Presents data covering the financial structure and operations on nonbank U.S. affiliates of foreign direct investors. Includes eight groups of tables—Group F, "Employment and employee compensation," covers employment and total employee compensation (wages and salaries) by industry of affiliate, and by country and industry of UBO (ultimate beneficial owner). *Foreign direct investment* also included in

the **CD-ROM** *National trade data bank (NTDB)*. C1.88:yr./mo./CD. monthly.

V.22.   *The state of small business; a report of the President transmitted to the Congress, together with the Annual report on small business and competition of the U.S. Small Business Administration.* Small Business Administra-tion. SBA 1.1/2:yr. annual.

Presents annual statistics and interpretation of small business trends including employment change. Contains supplementary tables on various areas of employment in small business which include tables on employment in selected small- and large-business dominated industries, and employment in selected indeterminate industries. Other tables include establishment employment by establishment size and major industry, and establishment employment by enterprise size and major industry.

V.23.   *U.S. industrial outlook; prospects for 350 industries with 450 tables and charts.* International Trade Administration. C 61.34:yr. annual.

Contains industry-by-industry analyses including historical data, current trends, forecasts of future prospects, international competitiveness, and industry statistical profiles. Analysis of each industry gives data for the past five years including employment, number of production workers where applicable, and their average hourly earnings. *U.S. industrial outlook* also included in the **CD-ROM** *National trade data bank (NTDB)*. C 1.88:yr./mo./CD. monthly.

Biennials, Triennials

V.24.   *Occupational outlook handbook.* BLS. L 2.3/4:yr. biennial. Provides detailed information on about 225 occupations. Occupations that require lengthy education or training are given the most attention. Includes employment statistics, salaries, and job outlook for each occupation. Supplemented by *Occupational outlook quarterly* (V.17), and *Occupational projections and training data* (V.25).

Occupational outlook handbook also available on CD-ROM. L 2.3/4-4:[yr.]CD.

V.25. *Occupational projections and training data, a statistical and research supplement to Occupational outlook handbook.* BLS. L 2.3/4-2:yr. biennial.
Provides statistics and technical data underlying the qualitative information presented in *Occupational outlook handbook* (V.24). Occupational employment projections usually cover 10 to 15 years. Gives current percentage of employees in occupations by age, sex, and race.

V.26. *Occupational employment in mining, construction, finance, and services.* BLS. L 2.3:2397. triennial.
Contains national data on occupational employment by SIC two-digit industries. Tables include statistics on employment, percent of total employment, and percent of establishments reporting the occupation. Description based on the 1990 survey.

V.27. *Occupational employment in selected nonmanufacturing industries.* BLS. L 2.3/16-2:yr. triennial.
Presents national data on occupational employment by SIC two-digit industries. Tables include statistics on employment, percent of total employment, and percent of establishments reporting the occupation.

Quinquennials, Decennials

V.28. *Economic censuses. Survey of minority-owned business enterprises. Asian Americans, American Indians, and other minorities.* Census Bureau. C 3.258:87-3. quinquennial.
Provides basic economic data on businesses owned by persons of American Indian, Asian, or other minority origin or descent. By major industry, gives number of firms, gross receipts, number of paid employees, and annual payroll. Data cover U.S. and individual states, and MSAs, counties, and places with 100 or more firms. Description based on the 1987 report.

V.29. *Economic censuses. Survey of minority-owned business enterprises. Black.* Census Bureau. C 3.258:87-1. quinquennial.
Provides basic economic data on businesses owned by blacks. Data include number of firms, gross receipts, number of paid employees, and annual payroll by major industry. Data cover U.S. and individual states, and MSAs, counties, and places with 100 or more black-owned firms. Description based on the 1987 report.

V.30. *Economic censuses. Survey of minority-owned business enterprises. Hispanic.* Census Bureau. C 3.258:87-2. quinquennial.
Provides basic economic data on businesses owned by Hispanics. Data include number of firms, gross receipts, number of paid employees, and annual payroll by major industry. Data cover U.S. and individual states, and MSAs, counties, and places with 100 or more Hispanic-owned firms. Description based on the report for 1987.

V.31. *Economic censuses. Survey of minority-owned business enterprises. Summary.* Census Bureau. C 3.258:87-4. quinquennial.
Summarizes the data in the three reports cited above: *Asian-Americans* (V.28), *Black* (V.29), and *Hispanic* (V.30). Description based on the 1987 report.

V.32. *Economic censuses. Women-owned businesses.* Census Bureau. C 3.250:WB 87-1. quinquennial.
Provides basic economic data on businesses owned by women. The published data cover number of firms, gross receipts, number of paid employees, and annual payroll by major industry. Geographic areas cover U.S. and individual states, and MSAs, counties, and places with 100 or more women-owned businesses. Description based on the 1987 report.

V.33. *Enterprise statistics. Company summary.* Census Bureau. C 3.230:ES 87-3. quinquennial.

Presents data for companies primarily engaged in mineral, construction, manufacturing, wholesale trade, retail trade, most service industries, and selected transportation industries. Data include number of companies, number of employees, annual payroll, sales, and receipts. Data are shown by Enterprise Industrial Classification (EIC) at the national level and by major industry for states. Description based on the 1987 report.

V.34.   *Enterprise statistics. Large companies.* Census Bureau. C 3.230:ES 87-1. quinquennial.

Presents data for companies with 500 or more employees primarily engaged in mineral industries, construction, manufacturing, wholesale trade, retail trade, most service industries, and selected transportation industries. Data include number of companies, number of employees, annual payroll, sales and receipts, and other applicable data. Data is shown by Enterprise industrial classification (EIC) at the national level. Description based on the 1987 report.

V.35.   *Census of population and housing. Equal employment opportunity file.* Census Bureau. C 3.283:CD 90-EEO-1-2. decennial.

Covers employment by detailed occupation by sex, race, and Hispanic origin for U.S., states, counties, and places of over 50,000.

Irregularly Updated Publications

V.36.   *Occupational employment in transportation, communications, utilities, and trade.* BLS. L 2.3:2220. irreg.

Presents national data on occupational employment by SIC two-digit code for these four industries. Trade covers wholesale and retail trade. Tables include statistics on employment, and percent of total employment. Description based on the 1985 survey.

Private Sector—Nonmanufacturing—Specific Industry

For documents dealing primarily with manufacturing, *see* Private Sector—Manufacturing on p. 77.

Agriculture

V.37.   *Agricultural statistics.* Agriculture Dept. A 1.47:yr. annual.
A reference book on agricultural production, supplies, consumption, facilities, costs, and returns. Consists of tables of annual data covering commonly used agricultural facts including employment and wages of agricultural workers in the U.S. and regions, also table on employment of farm workers by sex for the U.S.

V.38.   *Residents of farms and rural areas. Current population reports. Series P-20, no. Population characteristics.* Census Bureau. C 3.186:P-20/no. annual.
Presents a statistical portrait of the farm resident and rural populations of the United States. Information is primarily from the Current Population Survey (CPS).[1] Includes section, "Labor force participation," which gives employment of farm and nonfarm residents by age and sex; employment by occupation and industry of farm residents; and income and poverty status of farm and nonfarm residents. Previously published under the title *Rural and farm population.*

Construction Industry

V.39.   *Construction review.* Commerce Dept., International Trade Administration. C 61.37:yr. quarterly.
Brings together under one cover virtually all of the government's current statistics that pertain to construction. Each issue contains the section, "Contract construction employment," which includes data on number of employees by type of contractor, and gross hours and earnings of construction workers by type of contractor. *Construction review* is also included in the CD-ROM *National economic,*

social, and environmental data book (NESE DB). C 1.88/2:yr./no. quarterly.

V.40.   *Census of construction industries. Geographic area series.* C 3.245/7:CC 87-A-nos. Census Bureau. quinquennial. Series of ten reports on the construction industry, one report for each census division, and a U.S. summary. Gives number of establishments, employment, payroll, expenditures, and value of construction work, and other applicable data, by state and selected MSA. Description based on the 1987 edition.

V.41.   *Census of construction industries. Industry series.* Census Bureau. C 3.245/3:CC 92-I-nos. quinquennial. Series of 27 reports on the construction industry, one report for each of 26 industries and a U.S. summary. Classified at SIC four-digit level, each report gives number of establishments, employment, payroll, expenditures, value of construction work, and other applicable data for the U.S. and individual states. Description based on the 1992 edition.

Criminal Justice

V.42.   *Sourcebook of criminal justice statistics.* Justice Dept., Bureau of Justice Statistics. J 29.9/6:yr. annual. Brings together in a single volume nationwide data of interest to the criminal justice community. The scope of the data is national but includes considerable data on regions, states, counties, and cities. Gives employment statistics and payroll for police, judicial and legal services, corrections, and other judicial activities covering the U.S. and states, with totals for counties and municipalities in each state.

V.43.   *Children in custody: a comparison of public and private juvenile custody facilities.* Justice Dept., Office of Juvenile Justice and Delinquency Prevention. J 32.2:C 43/5/yr. biennial. Provides statistics on juveniles in custody by age and adjudication status, operating costs of facilities, and juvenile facility employees for public and private facilities by race (white, black, other), whether full time, part time, or volunteers.

Education

V.44.   *Condition of education.* National Center for Education Statistics. ED 1.109:yr./v.1-2. annual.

This two-volume set presents detailed data on the current condition of education in the U.S. Volume 1, "*Elementary and secondary education,*" includes tables on employment/unemployment rates of young adults (25-34) by years of school completed, and on ratio of median annual earnings of this same group by years of school completed. Other tables cover employment of teachers and administrators in public and private schools by sex, race, and Hispanic origin, and average annual and beginning salaries of teachers in public schools by sex, race, and Hispanic origin. Volume 2, "*Post secondary education,*" includes tables on median starting salaries of college graduates by field of study, average earnings of faculty by field of teaching, and number employed in higher education by occupation. Description based on 1991 edition.

V.45.   *Digest of education statistics.* National Center for Education Statistics. ED 1.310/2:yr.v.1-2. annual.

Provides a compilation of statistical information covering the broad field of American education from kindergarten through graduate school. Among the variety of subjects covered, gives employment of teachers in public and private elementary and secondary schools by state, and minimum and average salary of teachers by state. The same data is given for faculty in higher education institutions. Also includes tables on employment/unemployment, and income of the U.S. labor force by years of school completed. *Digest of education statistics* also included in the CD-ROM *National economic, social, and environmental data book (NESE DB).* C 1.88/2:yr./no. quarterly.

V.46.   *Projections of education statistics.* National Center for Education Statistics. ED 1.120:yr-yr. annual.
Provides statistics on elementary, secondary, and higher education at the national level for current and past years, and annual projections for the next 12 years, including statistics for elementary and secondary classroom teachers.

V.47.   *Salaries of full-time instructional faculty on 9- and 10-month contracts in institutions of higher education.* National Center for Education Statistics. ED 1.328/3: H 53/2. annual.
In addition to salary data, gives faculty employment by faculty, rank, and sex. Data are given for current year with trends of the last ten years.

V.48.   *State higher education profiles, a comparison of state higher education data.* National Center for Education Statistics. ED 1.116/3:yr. annual.
Survey on higher education enrollment, faculty, finances, and degrees in each state and the District of Columbia. Gives nationwide profile on average salary and number of full-time faculty by length of contract and academic rank.

V.49.   *State profiles of public elementary and secondary education.* National Center for Education Statistics. ED 1.328:   El 2/yr. biennial.
Gives public education profile for the U.S., each state, and five outlying areas. Each profile includes federal aid to education, enrollment by race and Hispanic origin, total education staff (instructional staff, support services staff, and administrators). States are ranked in "Rankings of States" tables by total number of students, number of classroom teachers, pupil-teacher ratio, number of administrators, average teacher salary, and other comparative data.

Fisheries

V.50. *Fisheries of the U.S.* National Marine Fisheries Service. C 55.309/2-2:yr. annual.

Annual compilation of data on the U.S. fishing industry. Includes employment by region and state.

Health Care

V.51. *Health care financing review.* Health and Human Services Dept., Health Care Financing Administration. HE 22.18:v./nos. quarterly with annual supplement.

Contains articles relating to health care financing. Each issue has table entitled "Health care indicators," which includes statistics on employment and earnings for private health service establishments by type of establishment for current and previous three quarters, and annually for the past three years. Also gives employment for all hospitals, both private and government.

V.52. *Health U.S., and prevention profile.* Public Health Service. HE 20.6223:yr. annual.

Presents statistics in over 140 detailed tables concerning recent trends in the health care sector, giving data for current and previous years. Includes tables of health care personnel by profession; separate tables on employment of physicians by region and state, and by activity; and employment in selected occupations in community hospitals and mental health organizations.

V.53. *Factbook: health personnel, U.S.* Dept. of Health and Human Services, Health Resources and Services Administration. biennial. This document is not printed by the Government Printing Office. For location, see *American statistics index,* 1993, fiche no. 4114-13.

This report first released in 1993 covers number of employed health professionals and enrollment in health professional schools. Data provided by health occupation.

Justice

see also Criminal Justice

V.54. *Justice expenditure and employment in the U.S.* Justice Dept., Bureau of Justice Statistics. J 29.11/2:yr. annual.

Series of statistical reports that present employment and expenditure data on civil and criminal justice activities in the U.S. These data are supplied by the federal government, each of the 50 state governments, and the aggregate local government within each state. The same data is given for 72 large county governments and 49 large city governments.

Law Enforcement

V.55.   *Uniform crime reports: crime in the U.S.* Federal Bureau of Investigation. J 1.14/7:yr. annual.
Annual statistical report on crime in the U.S. Includes section on law enforcement employees, covering officers and civilian employees for cities, urban and rural counties, and colleges and universities within each state. Also contains tables with the same type of data for state law enforcement employees for each state.

V.56.   *Sheriffs' departments; a LEMAS report.* Justice Dept., Office of Justice Programs, Bureau of Justice Statistics. J 29.11:Sh 5/yr. triennial.
This Law Enforcement Management and Administrative Statistics (LEMAS) report surveys a nationally representative sample of sheriffs' departments and provides data on expenditures, employment (sex, race, and Hispanic), salaries, functions, training and educational requirements, computerization, programs, and policies.

V.57.   *Profiles of state and local law enforcement agencies.* Justice Dept., Bureau of Justice Programs, Bureau of Justice Statistics. J 29.11:P 94/yr. irreg.
Contains data on state and local police departments based on the Law Enforcement Management and Administrative Statistics (LEMAS) survey. Includes information on operation, equipment, personnel (salaries, and percentage employment by sex, race, and Hispanic origin) and educational and training requirements. Title varies.

Lumber Industry

V.58. *Bulletin of hardwood market statistics.* U.S. Forest Service,
       A 13.79/3:yr./qtr. quarterly.
       Covers production, prices, and employment in the hardwood
       industry, and international trade in hardwood products.

Mineral Industry

Annuals

V.59. *Coal production.* Energy Dept., Energy Information
       Administration. E 3.11/7-3:yr. annual.
       Provides statistics on the coal mining industry, including
       tables on average number of miners working daily by coal
       producing region and state, and by type of mining.

V.60. *Mineral commodity summaries.* Interior Dept., Bureau of
       Mines. I 28.148:yr. annual.
       Summary report for 92 nonfuel mineral commodities. Profiles
       for each of the commodities cover domestic production,
       including employment, import tariffs, government stock pile
       status, and world resources.

V.61. *Minerals yearbook.* Mines Bureau. 3 vols. I 28.37:yr.
       annual.
       This three-volume set discusses the annual performance of
       the worldwide mineral industry. Volume 1, *Area reports:
       domestic,* contains chapters on the mineral industry of each
       of the 50 states, Puerto Rico, Northern Marianas, island
       posessions and trust territory. Includes data on employment
       and wages in mining for most states, especially those with
       sizable mineral resources.

Quinquennials

V.62. *Census of mineral industries. Geographic area series.*
       Census Bureau. C 3.216/2:MIC 87-A-nos.
       quinquennial.
       Series of nine reports on the mineral industry, one report for
       each census division. At SIC 2-4 digit level, each report gives

number of establishments, employment, payroll, capital expenditure, and other applicable data by state and county. Description based on the 1987 edition.

V.63. *Census of mineral industries. Industry series.* Census Bureau. C 3.216:MIC 92-I-no. quinquennial.
Series of 12 industry reports, each of which provides statistics for individual industries or groups of related industries. Gives number of establishments, employment, payroll, shipments, and other applicable data for U.S. and selected states. Description based on the 1992 edition.

V.64. *Census of mineral industries. Subject series. General summary.* Census Bureau. C 3.216/4:MIC 87-S-1. quinquennial.
Gives historical statistics, and industry and geographical statistics on the mineral industries. Employment statistics are included in all three sections. Description based on the 1987 edition.

Physicians

V.65. *Characteristics of physicians.* Health Resources and Services Administration. HE 20.6617:yr. approximately every three to four years.
Set of 54 reports, one for each state, the District of Columbia, Puerto Rico, the Virgin Islands, and Pacific Islands, on practicing physicians' characteristics. Data source is the AMA physician master file [5] Provides data on age and sex of physicians, their federal/non-federal employment, specialty, major professional activity, specialty board certification, and training and practice location.

Alabama HE 20.6617:Al 1b/yr.

Alaska HE 20.6617:Al 1s/yr.

Arizona HE 20.6617:Ar 4i/yr.

Arkansas HE 20.6617:Ar 4k/yr.

California HE 20.6617:C 12/yr.

Colorado HE 20.6617:C 71/yr.

Connecticut HE 20.6617:C 76/yr.

Delaware HE 20.6617:D 37/yr.

District of Columbia HE 20.6617:D 63/yr.

Florida HE 20.6617:F 66/yr.

Georgia HE 20.6617:G 29/yr.

Hawaii HE 20.6617:H 31/yr.

Idaho HE 20.6617:Id 1/yr.

Illinois HE 20.6617:Il 6/yr.

Indiana HE 20.6617:In 2/yr.

Iowa HE 20.6617:Io 9/yr.

Kansas HE 20.6617:K 13/yr.

Kentucky. HE 20.6617:K 41/yr.

Louisiana HE 20.6617:L 93/yr.

Maine HE 20.6617:M 28/yr.

Maryland HE 20.6617:M 36/yr.

Massachusetts HE 20.6617:M 38/yr.

Michigan HE 20.6617:M 58/yr.

Minnesota HE 20.6617:M 66/yr.

Mississippi HE 20.6617:M 69i/yr.

Missouri HE 20.6617:M 69o/yr.

Montana HE 20.6617:M 76/yr.

Nebraska HE 20.6617:N 27/yr.

Nevada HE 20.6617:N 41/yr.

New Hampshire HE 20.6617:N 42h/yr.

New Jersey HE 20.6617:N 42j/yr.

New Mexico HE 20.6617:N 42m/yr.

New York HE 20.6617:N 42y/yr.

North Carolina HE 20.6617:N 81c/yr.

North Dakota HE 20.6617:N 81d/yr.

Ohio HE 20.6617:Oh 3/yr.

Oklahoma HE 20.6617:Ok 4/yr.

Oregon HE 20.6617:Or 3/yr.

Pennsylvania HE 20.6617:P 38/yr.

Puerto Rico HE 20.6617:P 96/yr.

Rhode Island HE 20.6617:R 34/yr.

South Carolina HE 20.6617:So 8c/yr.

South Dakota HE 20.6617:So 8d/yr.

Tennessee HE 20.6617:T 25/yr.

Texas HE 20.6617:T 31/yr.

Utah HE 20.6617:Ut 1/yr.

Vermont HE 20.6617:V 59/yr.

Virginia HE 20.6617:V 81/yr.

Washington HE 20.6617:W 27/yr.

West Virginia HE 20.6617:W 52v/yr.

Wisconsin HE 20.6617:W 75/yr.

Wyoming HE 20.6617:W 99/yr.

Pacific Islands HE 20.6617:P 11/yr.

Virgin Islands HE 20.6617:V 81/yr.

Railroads

V.66.   *Annual report*. Railroad Retirement Board. RR 1.1: annual. Covers operations and finances of railroad retirement and unemployment insurance programs administered by the Railroad Retirement Board. Statistical tables focus on retirement, unemployment, and survivors' benefits but do include number of currently employed and unemployed in U.S. railroads.

Retail Trade

V.67.   *Census of retail trade. Geographic area series.* Census
Bureau. C 3.255/2:RC 92-A-nos. quinquennial.
Series of 52 reports on retail trade, one for each state and the
District of Columbia., and a U.S. summary. Classified by
SIC 2-4 digit industry, each report includes statistics on
establishments, sales, payroll, employment, and other
applicable data. State report gives summary statistics for
state, counties, and places with 2,500 inhabitants or more,
and summary statistics by SIC for MSAs and for counties
and places with 350 establishments or more. U.S. summary
gives the same data at the national level as well as
establishment and sales data for states and MSAs.
Description based on the 1992 edition.

Science and Technology

V.68.   *International science and technology data update.* National
Science Foundation. NS 1.52:yr. annual.
Covers research and development expenditures, science and
engineering personnel, and science and technology outputs
and impacts for the U.S. and selected foreign countries.
Section on personnel includes percentage of scientists and
engineers engaged in nonacademic employment by sector for
U.S. and major industrial countries, employment of scientists
and engineers in selected foreign countries. Also similar
tables for scientists and engineers in research and
development including their employment in foreign countries.
Gives tables on immigrant scientists and engineers in the U.S.
by country of origin.

V.69.   *Characteristics of doctoral scientists and engineers in the
U.S.* National Science Foundation. NS 1.22:D 65/yr.
biennial.
Presents data on the demographic and employment
characteristics of the nation's doctoral scientists and
engineers. Data include employment by field, age, sex, race
and Hispanic origin, employment sector, and primary work

activity; also unemployment by age, sex, race, and Hispanic origin.

V.70.   *Science and engineering indicators.* National Science Foundation, National Science Board. NS 1.28/2:yr. biennial. Overview of developments in science and engineering, including education, workforce, and research and development. Chapter on workforce gives data on employment/unemployment by degree field. Detailed tables in appendix cover employment by industry and occupation for current and selected past years. Other tables include doctoral scientists and engineers employed in research and development.

V.71.   *U.S. scientists and engineers.* National Science Foundation. NS 1.22/7:yr. biennial.
Includes employment statistics of scientists and engineers by field with breakdowns by employment status, sector of employment, and primary work activity.

V.72.   *Women and minorities in science and engineering.* National Science Foundation. NS 1.49:yr. biennial.
Presents information on the participation of women, racial/ethnic groups (white, African-American, Asian, Native American, and Hispanic), and physically disabled in science and engineering. Covers data for fields of physical sciences, environmental sciences, life sciences, engineering, and various subfields. Gives employment and average salaries by field, sex, and racial/ethnic group. Also includes tables on employment, underemployment, education, and SAT scores for scientists and engineers.

Scientists, engineers, and technicians in manufacturing industries: detailed statistical tables. see V.89.

V.73.   *Scientists, engineers, and technicians in nonmanufacturing industries: detailed statistical tables.* National Science Foundation. NS 1.22:Sci 2/15. triennial.
Provides estimates based on the Occupational Employment Survey (OES)[5] of scientists, engineers, and technicians

employed in nonmanufacturing industries, by industry and occupation.

V.74. *Scientists, engineers, and technicians in trade and regulated industries.* National Science Foundation. NS 1.22:Sci 2/11/yr. triennial.

Provides estimates based on the Occupational Employment Survey (OES)[5] of scientists, engineers, and technicians in retail and wholesale trade, communications, transportation, and public utilities, by detailed industry and occupation.

Service Industry

V.75. *Census of service industries. Geographic area series.* Census Bureau. C 3.257/2:SC 92-A-nos. quinquennial.

Series of 52 reports on service establishments, one report for each state and the District of Columbia, and a U.S. summary. Classified at SIC 2-4 digit level, each report includes data on establishments, receipts, payroll, and employment. State reports give summary statistics for state, counties, and places with 2,500 inhabitants or more, summary statistics by SIC code for MSAs, and for places with 350 establishments or more. Description based on 1992 edition.

Shipbuilding

V.76. *Report on survey of U.S. shipbuilding and repair facilities.* Dept. of Transportation, Maritime Administration. TD 11.25:yr. annual.

Reports on major shipbuilding, repair, and drydocking facilities. Includes data on shipyard employment and earnings.

Telecommunications

V.77. *Statistics of communications common carriers.* Federal Communications Commission. CC 1.35:yr. annual.

Contains financial and operating data of the telecommunications industry including telephone and telegraph companies, controlling companies, and

Communication Satellite Corporation. Includes employment and total employee compensation by company.

Timber

V.78.   *Timber sales program.* U.S. Forest Service. 3 v. annual. This document is not printed by the U.S. Government Printing Office. For location see *American statistics index,* fiche no. 1204-36.
Covers timber industry and operations by region, national forest, and state. Includes employment data for timber industry by state, region, and national forest.

Transportation

V.79.   *National transportation statistics: annual report.* Transportation Department, Research and Special Programs Administration. TD 10.9:yr. annual.
Summarizes selected transportation statistics from a wide variety of government and private sources. Includes data on employment and earnings in major sectors of transportation and of related industries for the past ten years.

V.80.   *Census of transportation. Geographic area series. Selected transportation industries. Summary.* Census Bureau. C 3.233/5:TC 87 A-1. quinquennial.
Covers basically three areas of the transportation industry: motor freight transportation and warehousing, water transportation, and transportation services. By SIC 2-digit code gives number of establishments, revenues, employment, and other applicable data for U.S., individual states, and MSAs. Description based on the 1987 edition.

V.81.   *Census of transportation. Subject series. Selected transportation industries. Miscellaneous subjects.* Census Bureau. C 3.233/5:TC 87 S-1. quinquennial.
Gives the same summary statistics for U.S. and individual states as does the *Geographic area series* (V.80). Other tables include employment statistics by employment and revenue size of establishments, by employment and revenue

size of firms, and by legal form of organization. Description based on 1987 edition.

Wholesale Trade

V.82.   *Census of wholesale trade. Geographic area series.* Census Bureau. C 3.256/2:WC 92 A-nos. quinquennial.

Series of 52 reports on wholesale trade, one report for each state and District of Columbia, and a U.S. summary. Classified by SIC 2-4 digit industry, each includes statistics on establishments, sales, payroll, employment, and other applicable data. State reports give summary statistics for state, counties, and places with 2,500 inhabitants or more, and summary statistics by SIC for counties and places with 200 establishments or more. U.S. summary gives the same data at the national level as well as establishments and sales for states and largest MSAs. Description based on the 1992 edition.

V.83.   *Census of wholesale trade. Subject series. Miscellaneous subjects.* Census Bureau. C 3.256/3:WC 87-S-4. quinquennial.

Contains data by kind of business and type of operation for the U.S. on sales by class of customer, employment by principal activity, detailed type of operation, and other applicable data. Description based on 1987 edition.

Private Sector—Manufacturing

Annuals

V.84.   *Annual survey of manufactures. Geographic area statistics.* Census Bureau. C 3.24/9-9:yr. annual.

Provides key measures of manufacturing activity for industry groups and important industries for intercensal years. Data include tables by SIC 2-3 digit industry on employment, hours, payrolls, and other applicable data for the U.S. and individual states.

V.85.   *Annual survey of manufactures. Statistics for industry groups and industries (including capital expenditures, inventories, and supplemental labor, fuel, and electric energy costs).* Census Bureau. C 3.24/9-7:yr. annual.
Annual data is presented for the U.S. by SIC 2-4 digit level on employment, hours, payroll, and other applicable data from a representative sample of about 55,000 establishments. Tables cover all employees, plus separate tables for production workers. This survey is conducted each year between the five-year *Census of manufactures industry series.* Provides key measures of manufacturing activity for industry groups and important industries for intercensal years.

V.86.   *Exports from manufacturing establishments. Manufacturing: analytical report series.* Census Bureau. C 3.24/9-12:yr-1. annual.
Provides estimates of the value of manufactured exports and export-related employment. Tables give value of manufacturers shipments and manufacturing employment related to manufactured exports for the U.S. and individual states by SIC 3-digit industry.

V.87.   *U.S. manufactured exports and export-related employment. Profiles of the 50 states and 35 selected metropolitan areas.* International Trade Administration. C 61.2:Ex 7/18/yr. annual.
Contains annual estimates of export-related sales and employment for each of the 50 states, the District of Columbia, and for 35 major metropolitan areas

Triennials

V.88.   *Occupational employment in manufacturing industries.* BLS. L 2.3/16:yr. triennial.
Presents national data on occupational employment by 2-digit SIC industries. Tables include statistics on employment, percent of total employment, and percent of establishments reporting the occupation.

V.89.   *Scientists, engineers, and technicians in manufacturing industries: detailed statistical tables*. National Science Foundation. NS 1.22:Sci 2/12/yr. triennial.

Provides estimates based on the Occupational Employment Survey (OES)[5] of scientists, engineers, and technicians employed in manufacturing industries.

Quinquennials

V.90.   *Census of manufactures. Geographic area series*. Census Bureau. C 3.24/3:MC 92-A-nos. quinquennial.

Series of 51 reports on manufactures, one for each state and District of Columbia. Classified by SIC 2-4 digit industry, each report includes employment, payroll, and other applicable data for state, MSA, and selected counties and places. Updated but with less detail than *Annual survey of manufactures. Geographic area statistics* (V.84). Description based on the 1992 report.

V.91.   *Census of manufactures. Industry series*. Census Bureau. C 3.24/4:MC 92-I-nos. quinquennial.

Series of 83 reports presents statistics for each of approximately 459 industries by groups of related SIC 4-digit industries. Each report gives number of establishments, number of employees, payroll, and other applicable data on industry groups for the U.S. and individual states. This entry and description covers the 1992 report of the Census of manufactures. It supersedes the *Census of manufactures Preliminary reports industry series* (C 3.24/8:MC 92-I-nos.(P)).

V.92.   *Census of manufactures. Subject series*. Census Bureau. C 3.24/12:MC[yr.]-S-nos. quinquennial.

Series of seven reports covering activities of manufacturing establishments. Only reports 1, 5, and 7 are applicable to this bibliography. The following entries and descriptions are based on reports of the 1987 census. No.1, *General summary: Industry product class, and Geographic area statistics*. Presents selected manufacturing industry data for the U.S. and individual states by SIC 2-4 digit industry. Includes summary statistics for all manufacturing establishments by state, and selected statistics for manufacturing establishments by state and metropolitan area. Statistics include number of establishments, number of employees, number of production workers, and other applicable data.

No. 5, *Type of organization.* Gives manufacturing statistics by type of organization (type of company ownership and legal form of organization) for major industry groups and SIC 4-digit industry. Statistics include number of establishments, total number of employees, number of production workers, and other key manufacturing data. Separate tables for the U.S. and each state.

No. 7, *Manufacturers shipments to the federal government.* Provides data by SIC 4-digit industry and includes number of employees and value of shipments to the federal government, with the same data covering individual agencies: DOD, NASA, DOE. Also reports on employees involved in government shipments by type of government contract.

V.93.   *Selected characteristics of manufacturing establishments that export. Manufacturing: analytical report series.* Census Bureau. C 3.24/9-12:[yr.]-2. quinquennial.

Based on export activity data reported by manufacturing establishments for the quinquennial *Census of manufactures.* Tables are by SIC 2-digit industry for the U.S. and individual states and cover number of exporting establishments, shipments, and employment related to manufactured exports by employment size of establishment, and export intensity of exporting establishments by employment size of establishment. Entry and description based on report from the 1987 *Census of manufactures.*

Private Sector—Manufacturing—Specific Industry

Automobile Industry

V.94.   *Annual report of the President to the Congress on the operation of the Automotive Products Trade Act of 1965.* International Trade Administration. annual. This document is not printed by the U.S. Government Printing Office. For location see *American Statistics Index,* fiche no. 2044-35. Report on the automotive trade between U.S. and Canada, and operation of the Automotive Trade Products Act. Includes production, sales, exports and imports, and gives total employment for the U.S. and Canadian automotive products industry.

V.95.   *U.S. automobile industry monthly report on selected economic indicators.* U.S. International Trade Commission. ITC 1.16/3:yr./no. monthly.
Provides data on the U.S.'s new automobile industry including production, sales, and employment.

Steel Industry

V.96.   *Quarterly report on the status of the steel industry. Report to the Committee on Ways and Means on Investigation no.332-226 under section 332 of the Tariff act of 1930.* International Trade Administration. ITC 1.27:date. quarterly.
Provides data on the U.S. steel imports by country, and U.S. steel industry operations and finances, including tables on employment and wages in the steel industry.

Chapter Six

Income/Earnings—
General Sources

VI.1. *Compensation and working conditions.* BLS, Office of Compensation and Working Conditions. L 2.44:v./no. monthly.

Reports on employee compensation, including wages, salaries, benefits, and other aspects of the work environment such as safety and health. Presents wage and benefit changes resulting from collective bargaining settlements and unilateral management decisions; statistical summaries by major industry, excluding agriculture; and special reports on wage trends. Previously published under the title *Current wage developments.*

VI.2. *News. Usual weekly earnings of wage and salary workers.* BLS. L 2.126:yr./no. quarterly.

Each issue has statement on developments in earnings for wage and salary workers for that particular quarter. Tables on median weekly earnings are given by age, sex, race, and Hispanic origin; also median weekly earnings by major occupation and sex, and for part-time workers by age, sex, race, and Hispanic origin. Previously published under the title *Weekly earnings of wage and salary workers.*

VI.3. *Local area personal income.* Commerce Dept., Bureau of Economic Analysis. C 59.18:yr.-yr./v.1-5. annual. RRG 2.

Estimates in this five-volume study constitute one of the most extensive bodies of annual economic information that is available for the nation's counties and metropolitan areas.

Corresponding data is given for the U.S. and each state. The personal estimates presented in these volumes cover the most recent year and the preceding five years. It is divided into five volumes: v.1. *Summary.* v.2. *New England, Mideast and Great Lakes.* v.3. *Plains region.* v.4. *Southeast region.* v.5. *Southwest, Rocky Mountain and Far West regions, Alaska and Hawaii.* Discontinued with issue covering the years 1984-89. Similar data continued on CD-ROM *Regional economic information system* (VI.5A).

VI.4. *Money income and poverty status in the United States. Current population reports. Series P-60. Consumer income.* Census Bureau. C 3.186/11:yr. annual. RRG 2.
Presents data on the income and poverty status of households, families, and persons in the U.S. for the current year with some comparative data for earlier years. Data compiled from the Current Population Survey (CPS).[1]

VI.5. *Money income of households, families and persons in the United States.* Census Bureau. C 3.186/2:yr. annual. RRG 2.
Presents detailed data on the income of households, families, and persons in the United States for the current year with some comparative data for earlier years. Data was compiled from the annual Current Population Survey (CPS).[1]

VI.5A. *Regional economic information system, 1969-91.* Bureau of Economic Analysis. C 59.24:yr. CD. annual. RRG 2.
Presents local area estimates of personal income and employment for selected years from 1969 to date, by region, state, county, and MSA, and by SIC 1-2 digit industry. Description based on report released in 1993.

VI.6. *Local population estimates. Population and per capita income estimates for counties and incorporated places. Current population reports. Series P-26.* Census Bureau. biennial. RRG 2.
Contains annual population estimates and annual estimates of per capita income for all general purpose governmental units

within each state. Governmental units included in this report are (1) counties (or county equivalents), (2) incorporated places, (3) active minor civil divisions or townships. Divided into five reports by census region:

Northeast C 3.186/27:yr.
West C 3.186/27-2:yr.
West North Central C 3.186/27-3:yr.
East North Central C 3.186/27-4:yr.
South C 3.186/27-5:yr.

These biennial reports were previously published separately for each state.

VI.7 *Income, poverty, and wealth in the United States: a chartbook. Current population reports. Consumer income, Series P-60.* Census Bureau. C 3.186:P 60/179. irreg. Includes data on income of households, families, and persons in the U.S. Section on poverty in the U.S. covers social and economic characteristics of the population below the poverty level. Another section presents data on household wealth and asset ownership. Description based on report issued in 1992.

VI.8. *State personal income: 1929-(yr.); estimates and a statement of sources and methods.* Commerce Dept., Bureau of Economic Analysis. C 59.2:In 2/4/yr. irreg., approximately every five years. RRG 2.
Presents the full set of state personal income estimates. The tables show the following estimates for each state and for the eight regions and the United States: Annual total and per capita personal income for 1929-yr.; annual total and per capita disposable income for 1948-yr.; annual personal income by major type of payment and by industry for 1929-yr.; and quarterly total personal income for 1969-yr. Description based on report covering 1929-87, issued 1989.

VI.9. *Trends in income, by selected characteristics: 1947-(yr.) Current population reports. Series P-60. Consumer income.* Census Bureau. C 3.186:P 60/167. irreg. RRG 2.
This report primarily examines the median incomes of

households, families, and persons over time by a variety of characteristics. Income estimates are shown in both current and constant dollars. This report is unique in the P 60 series in that it gives historical income statistics compiled from previous reports in the P 60 series. Description based on report covering 1947-1988, issued 1990.

Chapter Seven

Income/Earnings—
Separate Reports on Minorities, Ancestry Groups, Women, and Special Population Groups

Minorities

African-Americans

VII.1. *Black news digest: news from the United States Dept. of Labor, Office of Information and Public Affairs.* The Office. L 1.20/6:date. weekly.
This newsletter contains articles and statistics on black Americans in the labor force, as well as on the labor force in general. Each quarter gives median weekly earnings by age, sex, and race.

VII.2. *The Black population in the United States. Current population reports. Series P-20. Population characteristics.* Census Bureau. C 3.186:P 20/no. annual.
Presents statistical portrait of the demographic, social, and economic status of blacks based on the Current Population Survey (CPS).[1] Gives tables on employment, unemployment, and income by sex and race (white, black).

VII.2A. *Census of population.* [*Population subject reports*] *Characteristics of the black population.* Census Bureau. C 3.223/10:990 CP-3-6. decennial.
Data in these detailed and comprehensive subject reports on blacks are taken from the decennial census of population.

They cover population, social, labor force, economic, and housing characteristics for black Americans. Economic characteristics include data on income and poverty status.

VII.3. *We the American... Blacks.* Census Bureau. C 3.2:Am 3/14. decennial.

Concise information booklets on black Americans with data provided by the decennial census of population and housing. Includes population, social, and economic data. Economic characteristics cover occupations, income, and poverty rates. Most of the data is given in graphic form.

Asian and Pacific Islander Americans

VII.4. *Census of population. [Population subject reports]. Asians and Pacific Islanders in the United States.* Census Bureau. C 3.223/10:990 CP-3-5. decennial.

Data in these detailed and comprehensive subject reports on Asians and Pacific Islanders are taken from the decennial census of population. They cover population, social, labor force, economic, and housing characteristics for all Asians and for specific Asian and Pacific Islander groups, e.g., Chinese, Filipino, Japanese, etc. Economic characteristics include data on income and poverty status. This subject report is also available on CD-ROM under the title: *Characteristics of the Asian and Pacific Islander population in the United States.* C 3.286:CD 90 SSTF 05.

VII.5. *We the American... Asians.* Census Bureau. C 3.2:Am 3/13. decennial.

Concise information booklets on Asian-Americans with data provided by the decennial census of population and housing. Includes population, social, and economic data. Economic data include occupation, income, and poverty level. Provides these statistics for all Asians as well as for specific Asian origin groups, e.g., Chinese, Filipino, Japanese, etc.

VII.6. *We the American... Pacific Islanders.* Census Bureau. C 3.2: Am 3/15. decennial.

Concise information booklets on Pacific Islander Americans with data provided by the decennial census of population and housing. Tables cover social and economic characteristics which include occupation, income, and poverty level. Provides data for all Pacific Islander Americans as well as for specific Pacific Islander origin groups, e.g., Hawaiian, Samoan, Tongan, etc.

VII.7. *Asian and Pacific Islander population in the United States. Current population reports. Population characteristics.* Census Bureau. C 3.186:P 20/459. irreg.

Issued in 1992, this presents the first Current Population Survey[1] report on the demographic, social, and economic characteristics of the Asian and Pacific Islander population in the United States. Gives earnings statistics for the total population, Asian and Pacific Islander, and white population. Also shows earnings of Asians and Pacific Islanders by years of school completed. Information in this report is based on data from the March 1991 and 1990 supplements to the Current Population Survey (CPS).[1]

Hispanic Americans

VII.8. *The Hispanic population in the United States. Current population reports. Series P-20. Population characteristics.* Census Bureau. C 3.186/14-2:yr. annual.

Presents data on the demographic, social, and economic characteristics of the Hispanic population and its subgroups: Mexican, Puerto Rican, Cuban, Central and South American, and other Spanish origin groups. Includes detailed tables on employment, unemployment, and income.

VII.9. *Census of population. [Population subject reports]. Persons of Hispanic origin in the United States.* Census Bureau. C 3.223/10:990 CP-3-3. decennial.

Data in these detailed and comprehensive subject reports on Hispanics are taken from the decennial census of population. They cover population, social, labor force, economic, and housing characteristics for all Hispanics, and for specific

Hispanic origin groups, e.g., Chilean, El Salvadoran, Mexican, etc. Economic characteristics include data on income and poverty status. *Persons of Hispanic origin in the United States* also available on CD-ROM: C 3.286:CD 90 SSTF 03.

VII.9A. *We the American... Hispanics.* Census Bureau. C 3.2:Am 3/18. decennial.

Concise information booklets on Hispanic Americans with data provided by the decennial census of population and housing. Tables cover social and economic characteristics which include occupation, income, and poverty status. Provides data for all Hispanic Americans as well as for specific Hispanic origin groups, e.g., Cuban, Mexican, Puerto Rican, etc.

Indians of North America

VII.9B. *Census of population. [Population subject reports]. Characteristics of American Indians by tribe and language.* Census Bureau. C 3.223/10:990 CP-3-7/sec.1-2. decennial.

Data in these detailed and comprehensive subject reports on American Indians are taken from the decennial census of population. They include income and poverty status for the U.S., individual states, and metropolitan areas, by Indian tribe.

VII.10. *Census of population. Social and economic characteristics. American Indian and Alaska native areas.* Census Bureau. C 3.223/7-2:990 CP-2-1A/sec.1-2. decennial.

This report on American Indian and Alaskan native areas appears separately for the first time in the 1990 census. In 1980 the data appeared in the series *General social and economic characteristics.* Covers detailed social and economic characteristics of American Indian, Eskimo, or Aleut persons. Tables provide data for individual American Indian reservations and trust lands, and Alaska native village areas, with county and state parts for each individual area.

Includes income and poverty status by sex, and by age for persons 60 years and over.

VII.11. *We the first... Americans.* Census Bureau. C 3.2:Am 3/19. decennial.

Concise information booklets on American Indians and Alaska natives with data provided by the decennial census of population and housing. Data are given for American Indians, Eskimos, and Aleuts and include median family income and poverty rate. Most of the information is given in graphic form.

Ancestry and Foreign Born

VII.12. *Census of population. [Population subject reports]. Ancestry of the population in the United States.* Census Bureau. C 3.223/10:990 CP-3-2. decennial.

Data in these detailed and comprehensive subject reports on ancestry groups are taken from the decennial census of population. Provides population, housing, social, and economic characteristics on the ancestry and on the foreign born of the U.S. population. Economic characteristics include income and poverty status. All tables provide data on ancestry groups, and on foreign born by nativity, citizenship, and year of entry. *Ancestry of the population in the United States* also available on CD-ROM. C 3.286:CD 90 SSTF 02.

VII.13. *Census of population. [Population subject reports]. The foreign-born population in the United States.* Census Bureau. C 3.223/10:990 CP-3-1. decennial.

Data in these detailed and comprehensive reports on the foreign-born population in the United States are taken from the decennial census of population. They include general population and housing characteristics, social and labor force characteristics, and income and poverty status of the foreign born. All tables are cross indexed by nativity, citizenship, and year of entry. This subject report on the foreign born is issued for the first time by the census of population, 1990. *The foreign-born population in the United States* also available on **CD-ROM**: C 3.286:CD 90 SSTF 01.

VII.14. *We the American...foreign born*. Census Bureau. C 3.2: Am 3/21/yr. decennial.

Concise information booklets on America's foreign born with data provided by the decennial census of population and housing. Gives data on total foreign born and more detailed data on immigrants of the 11 countries that provide the highest number of foreign born. Data on immigrants from these countries include income and poverty level.

Women

VII.15. *Women & work: news from the U.S. Dept. of Labor, Office of Information, Publications and Reports*. The Office. L 1.20/8:date. monthly.

Covers articles of interest for women and for the population as a whole on the current labor situation. Periodically gives median weekly earnings by age, sex, race, and Hispanic origin. Also shows these same earnings by major occupation and sex.

VII.16. *We the American...women*. Census Bureau. C 3.2:Am 3/6/yr. decennial.

Concise information booklets on American women with data provided by the decennial Census of population and housing. They include median family income with female householder, and poverty rates of persons by age and sex. Most of the information is given in graphic form.

VII.17. *Facts on working women*. Labor Dept., Women's Bureau. L 36.114/3:yr./no. irreg., usually several issues per year.

A series of pamphlets, each one dealing with a specific aspect of women in the labor force. Statistical tables are included in most pamphlets. Some examples of recent titles: *Earnings differences between women and men; Black women in the labor force;* and *Women workers outlook to 2005.*

VII.18. *Working women: a chartbook.* BLS. L 2.3:2385. irreg.
Chartbook on women in the labor force giving comparisons to
men from 1960-1990. Gives earnings by age, race, and
Hispanic origin. Description based on 1991 edition.

Special Population Groups

Aged

VII.19. *Income of the aged: a chartbook.* Social Security
Administration. HE 3.2:In 2/6/yr. biennial.
Includes median income and income sources for persons 65
and over. Other data include poverty status and income by
age groups, sex, race, and Hispanic origin.

VII.20. *Income of the population 55 or older.* Social Security
Administration. HE 3.75:yr. biennial.
Gives income sources and median income for all persons 55
or older by age, sex, race, and Hispanic origin.

VII.21. *Census of population and housing. Special tabulation on
aging.* Census Bureau. C 3.281/2:CD 90-AOA1. decennial.
This CD-ROM product issued for the first time by the 1990
census of population and housing gives income and poverty
status of persons by age from 45-85, and of families, by
state, county, metropolitan area, city, and places of 2,500 or
more.

VII.22. *Aging America, trends and projections.* Prepared by the U.S.
Senate Special Committee on Aging, the American
Association of Retired Persons, the Federal Council on the
Aging, and the U.S. Administration on Aging. Y 3.F 31/15:
Ag 4/2/yr. irreg.
Analyzes demographic and socioeconomic trends on the aged
population (65 and over) in the U.S., including a section on
the aged in selected countries. Gives current and retrospective
data on income and labor force participation. Description
based on 1991 edition.

Disabled

VII.23. *Chartbook on work disability in the United States.* Education Dept., National Institute on Disability and Rehabilitation Research. ED 1.2:D 63/8/yr. irreg.

A reference book on work disability in the U.S. Section 5, "Work disability, income and earnings," gives average earnings and median annual income by sex, rates on poverty status, and sources of income and benefits (social security, public housing, etc.).

VII.24. *Labor force status and other characteristics of persons with a work disability: 1981-88. Current population reports. Series P 23, no.160.* Census Bureau. C 3.186:P 23/no. 160. irreg.

Provides data on characteristics of persons with a work disability, including earnings by sex, race, and Hispanic origin. Comparative statistics are given for two groups: those with a severe disability and those with a disability which is not severe. Comparative statistics are also given for the population without a work disability.

Education—Income by Educational Status

VII.25. *Educational attainment in the United States.* Census Bureau. C 3.186/23:yr. annual.

Gives data on the educational attainment of persons in the United States from the Current Population Survey (CPS).[1] Detailed tables on years of school completed with median earnings and income by age, sex, race, and Hispanic origin.

VII.26. *Census of population. [Population subject reports]. Education in the United States.* Census Bureau. C 3.223/10:990 CP-3-4. decennial.

Data in these detailed and comprehensive reports on education are taken from the decennial census of population. They provide statistics on educational attainment by age, sex, race, and Hispanic origin for the U.S. and individual states.

Include mean annual earnings by educational attainment for the U.S. and each state by sex. race, and Hispanic origin.

VII.27. *What's it worth? Educational background and economic status. Current population reports. Series P-70, no. Household economic status.* Census Bureau. C 3.186: P-70/2/no. irreg., approximately every three years.
Covers the relationship between education and income. Tables give income by degree and years of schooling by age, also income by field of degree, e.g., agriculture, engineering, psychology.

Poor

VII.28. *Poverty in the United States. Current population reports. Series P-60. Consumer income series.* Census Bureau. C 3.186/22:yr. annual.
Presents social and economic characteristics of the population below the poverty level based on the Current Population Survey (CPS).[1] Tables give poverty status by age, sex, race, and Hispanic origin. Other tables give poverty status by education, work experience, and disability.

Retirees

VII.29. *Pensions, worker coverage and retirement benefits. Household economic studies. Series P-70.* Census Bureau. C 3.186:P-70/2/no. irreg.
Presents data from the Survey of Income and Program Participation (SIPP).[7] Discusses the issues of pension eligibility of the working population and characteristics of persons receiving retirement income. Tables include number of wage and salary workers by pension status, number of pension recipients giving mean pension and social security income, cross tabulated by age, sex, race, and Hispanic origin, and by education and major industry. Description based on report from SIPP conducted in 1987, issued 1991.

Social Security Recipients

VII.30. *Social security bulletin.* Social Security Administration, Office of Research and Statistics. HE 3.3:v.nos.&nos. monthly.

Reports current data and analysis pertinent to the social security program. Gives monthly and quarterly statistics on current social security programs. Also includes historical data from 1940 or year of program initiation. Gives number of persons receiving benefits and average amount of monthly benefits. Programs include OASDI cash benefits, Supplementary Security Income, Public Assistance, and Unemployment Insurance. Except for OASDI, these programs are analyzed by state.

VII.31. *OASDI beneficiaries by state and county.* Social Security Administration, Office of Research and Statistics. HE 3.73/2:yr. annual.

Presents information by state and county on the number of persons who received social security benefits under the Old-Age Survivors, and Disability Insurance (OASDI) program. All tables give type of benefit (retirement, survivor, etc.) and type of beneficiary (retired, widows and widowers, etc.). Table 5 gives total beneficiary payments for state and county.

VII.32. *Social security bulletin, annual statistical supplement.* Social Security Administration, Office of Policy. HE 3.3/3:yr. annual.

Tables in this annual supplement augment the monthly and quarterly tables carried in the regular issues of the *Bulletin* (VII.30) with tables cross indexed by age, sex, and race.

VII.33. *SSI recipients by state and county.* Social Security Administration, Office of Research and Statistics. HE 3.71:yr. annual.

Presents information by state and county on the Supplemental Security Income (SSI) program. The tables show the number of recipients of federal SSI and federally administered state supplementation payments by reason for eligibility (aged, blind, or disabled). Table 6 gives total monthly SSI payments for state and county.

Refugees

VII.34. *Refugee Resettlement Program; report to the Congress.* Social Security Administration, Family Support Administration. annual. This document is not printed by the Government Printing Office. For location see *American statistics index,* fiche no. 4694-5.

Report on refugee resettlement program activities and funding. Includes tables on incomes received, including cash assistance recipients.

Trade Union Workers

VII.35. *News. Union members.* BLS. L 2.120/2-l2:yr. annual. Press release gives weekly earnings of union and nonunion workers by age, sex, race, and Hispanic origin, and by major industry and major occupation.

Youth

VII.36. *Youth indicators: trends in the well-being of American youth.* Education Dept., Office of Education Research and Improvement. ED 1.327:yr. irreg.

Compilation of largely statistical data on the youth population through age 24. Includes chapter on youth employment and income, and another on family income. Description based on 1991 edition.

Chapter Eight

Income/Earnings by Industry/Occupation

Public Sector (Government)

Federal Government

VIII.1. *Annual report on the employment of minorities, women, and people with disabilities in the federal government.* EEOC. Y 3.Eq 2:12-5/yr. annual.
Gives tables for department or agency on pay grade by sex, race, and Hispanic origin. Similar tables are given for handicapped employees.

VIII.2. *Pay structure of the federal civil service.* Federal civilian workforce statistics. OPM. PM 1.10/2:P 29/yr. annual.
Provides statistics on salary or wages of full-time federal civilian employees for the U.S., Washington, D.C., and overseas. Tables provide employment and wage data by agency pay system. Number of employees and average salaries and pay systems are given for states and MSAs. Employees of certain governmental units are excluded from this report, e.g., Congress, CIA, USPS.

VIII.3. *Salary tables [for] executive branch of the government.* OPM. PM 1.9:no. annual.
Includes five salary tables: "General schedule salary table," "Supplemental general schedule table", and "Special pay adjustments for law enforcement officers" (three salary tables). Each of the five tables give salaries for each GS grade and step, arranged from the lowest to the highest rate.

VIII.4. *Occupations of federal white-collar and blue-collar workers.* Federal civilian workforce statistics. OPM. PM 1.10/2-2:yr. biennial.
Provides data on federal full-time civilian white- and blue-collar workers. Tables are given by occupation, grade or salary range, agency, pay system, sex, and major geographic area (U.S., Washington, D.C., MSA, and overseas). Employment summaries are given for white- and blue-collar employment. Employees of certain governmental units (Congress, CIA, USPS) are excluded from this report.

State, County, and Local Governments

VIII.5. *City employment. Government employment:GE;yr.-no.2.* Census Bureau. C 3.140/2-3:yr. annual.
Provides statistics on municipal government employment, average earnings of employees, and payrolls for individual cities with 50,000 or more population by governmental function, for the month of October each year

VIII.6. *County government employment. Government employment: GE;yr.-no.4.* Census Bureau. C 3.140/2-5:yr. annual.
Provides statistics on county government employment, average earnings of employees, and payroll by governmental function, for the month of October each year.

VIII.7. *Job patterns for minorities and women in state and local government.* EEOC. Y 3.Eq 2:12-4/yr. annual.
Chiefly statistical tables on employment and salaries in state and local government by age, sex, race, and Hispanic origin. Tables cover national, state, and local summaries, with separate summaries for each state, also summaries by major job categories and govern-mental function.

VIII.8. *Public employment. Government employment:GE;yr.-no.1.* Census Bureau. C 3.140/2-4:yr. annual.
Provides state-by-state statistics with comparisons to local government, on employment and payroll, and average earnings by governmental function.

VIII.9. *Census of governments*. Census Bureau. C 3.145/4:yr/ v.1-4/nos. quinquennial.

A four-volume set with multiple parts to each volume covering four major subject fields: government organiza-tion, taxable property values, public employment, and government finances. Volume 3, *Public employment*, covers employment and earnings and will therefore be the only one described here. Vol. 3, no. 1, covers employment and average earnings of employees of major local governments. Vol. 3, no. 2, covers employment and average earnings of employees of state and local governments by function.

Private Sector—General Sources

VIII.10. *News. Employment and wages in foreign-owned businesses in the United States*. BLS. L 2.41/12: quarterly.

This news release gives average monthly employment and wages of foreign-owned U.S. establishments and all U.S. establishments by 50 four-digit SIC industries. Also employment and wages by state and major industry division. Additional tables cover employment and wages of foreign-owned U.S. establishments in selected countries, and employment and wages by major industry and country of ultimate beneficial owner.

VIII.10A.*Career guide to industries*. BLS. L 2.3/4-3:yr. annual.

A companion publication to *Occupational outlook handbook* (VIII.15), the *Guide* provides information on careers from an industrial perspective. Arranged by industry, gives current average earnings for selected occupations for most industries.

VIII.11. *Occupational compensation survey*. BLS. L 2.121/no.: no./yr. annual. RRG 2.

Covers occupational earnings and employment benefits for 90 metropolitan areas. Limited to establishments of 50 employees or more, the 32 largest metro areas are surveyed each year and two groups of 29 areas are surveyed in alternate years. Prior to 1990, 70 metro areas were surveyed annually. Includes reports on earnings for occupations common to a wide variety of establishments within six broad industry divisions. Industries excluded from the survey are government operations, construction, and extractive industries. Coverage includes office clerical, professional and technical, maintenance, custodial, and material movement occupations. Separate reports are issued for each metropolitan area. They are given an alpha-numeric classification, alphabetically by state, then alphabetically by metropolitan area within each state. They are listed here alphabetically by metropolitan area. Previously published under the title *Area wage survey.*

Anaheim-Santa Ana, CA L 2.121/5:An 1/yr. annual.

Appleton-Oshkosh-Neenah, WI L 2.121/49:Ap 5/yr.

Atlanta, GA L 2.121/10:At 6/yr. annual.

Augusta, GA-South Carolina. L 2.121/10:Au 4/yr.

Austin, TX L 2.121/43:Au 7/yr.

Baltimore, MD L 2.121/10:B 21/yr. annual.

Bergen-Passaic, NJ L 2.121/30:B 45/yr. annual.

Billings, MT L 2.121/26:B 49/yr.

Boise City, ID L 2.121/12:B 63/yr.

Boston, MA L 2.121/21:B 65/yr. annual.

Bradenton, FL L 2.121/9:B 72/yr.

Buffalo, NY L 2.121.32:B 86/yr.

Champaign-Urbana-Rantoul, IL L 2.121/13:C 35

Charleston, SC L 2.121/40:C 38

Chicago, IL L 2.121/13:C 43/yr. annual.

Cincinnati, OH-KY-IN L 2.121/35:C 49/yr.

Cleveland, OH L 2.121/35:C 59/yr. annual.

Columbus, OH L 2.121/35:C 72/yr.

Corpus Christi, TX L 2.121/43:C 81/yr.

Dallas-Fort Worth, TX L 2.121/43:D 16/yr. annual.

Danbury, CT L 2.121/7:D 19/yr.

Davenport-Rock Island-Moline, IO-IL
    L 2.121/15:D 27/yr.

Decatur, IL L 2.121/13:D 35/yr.

Denver-Boulder, CO L 2.121/6:D 43/yr. annual.

Detroit, MI L 2.121/22:D 48/yr. annual.

Elkhart-Goshen, IN L 2.121/14:El 5/yr.

Florence, SC L 2.121/40:F 66/yr.

Fresno, CA L 2.121/5:F 89/yr.

Gainesville, FL L 2.121/9:G 12/yr.

Gary-Hammond, IN L 2.121/14:G 19/yr.

Hartford, CT L 2.121/7:H 25/yr.

Houston, TX L 2.121/43:H 81/yr.

Huntsville, AL L 2.121/1:H 92/yr.

Indianapolis, IN L 2.121/14:In 2/yr.

Jackson, MS L 2.121/24:J 13/yr.

Joliet, IL L 2.121/13:J 68/yr.

Kansas City, MO-KS L 2.121/25:K 13/yr. annual.

Kokomo, IN L 2.121/14:K 82/yr.

Lawrence-Haverhill, MA-NH L 2.121/21:L 43/yr.

Little Rock-North Little Rock, AR L 2.121/4:L 72/yr.

Longview-Marshall, TX L 2.121/43:L 86/yr.

Los Angeles-Long Beach, CA L 2.121/5:L 89/yr. annual.

Louisville, KY-IN L 2.121/17:L 93/yr.

Memphis, TN-AR-MS L 2.121/42:M 51/yr.

Miami-Hialeah, FL L 2.121/9:M 58/yr. annual.

Middlesex-Somerset-Hunterdon, NJ
    L 2.121/20:M 58/yr.

Milwaukee, WI L 2.121/49:M 64/yr. annual.

Minneapolis-St. Paul, MN-WI L 2.121/23:M 66/yr.

Mobile, AL L 2.121/1:M 71/yr.

Monmouth-Ocean, NJ L 2.121/30:M 75/yr.

Nashville, TN L 2.121/42:N 17/yr.

Nassau-Suffolk, NY L 2.121/32:N 18/yr. annual.

New Orleans, LA L 2.121/18:N 42/yr. annual.

New York, NY L 2.121/32:N 42y/yr. annual.

Newark, NJ L 2.121/30:N 42/yr.

Oakland, CA L 2.121/5:Oa 4/yr. annual.

Omaha, NE-IA L 2.121/27:Om 1/yr.

Orlando, FL L 2.121/9:Or 5

Pawtucket-Woonsocket-Attleboro, RI-MA
    L 2.121/39:P 28

Philadelphia, PA-NJ L 2.121/38:P 53/yr. annual.

Phoenix, AZ L 2.121/3:P 56/yr. annual.

Pittsburgh, PA L 2.121/38:P 68/yr. annual.

Portland, ME L 2.121/19:P 83/yr.

Portland, OR L 2.121/27:P 83/yr.

Poughkeepsie, NY L 2.121/32:P 86/yr.

Richmond-Petersburg, VA L 2.121/46:R 41/yr.

Riverside-San Bernardino, CA L 2.121/5:R 52/yr.

Rochester, NY L 2.121/32:R 58/yr.

Salt Lake City-Ogden, UT L 2.121/44:Sa 3/yr.

San Angelo, TX L 2.121/43:Sa 5a/yr.

San Antonio, TX L 2.121/43:Sa 5a/2/yr.

San Diego, CA L 2.121/5:Sa 5/3/yr. annual.

San Francisco, CA L 2.121/5:Sa 5f/yr. annual.

San Jose, CA L 2.121/5:Sa 5j/yr. annual.

Scranton-Wilkes-Barre, PA L 2.121/38:Scr 1/yr.

Seattle, WA L 2.121/47:Se 1/yr. annual.

Shreveport, LA L 2.121/18:Sh 8/yr.

St. Cloud, MN L 2.121/23:Sa 2c/yr.

St. Louis, MO-IL L 2.121/25:Sa 2l/yr.

Tampa-St. Petersburg-Clearwater, FL
    L 2.121/9:T 15/yr.

Toledo, OH L 2.121/35:T 57/yr.

Trenton, NJ L 2.121/30:T 72/yr.

Visalia-Tulare-Porterville, CA L 2.121/5:V 82/yr.

Washington, DC-MD-VA L 2.121/51:D 63/yr. annual.

Wilmington, DE-NJ-MD
    L 2.121/8:W 68/yr.

Worcester, MS L 2.121/21:W 89/yr.

York, PA L 2.121/38:Y 8/yr.

VIII.12.*Occupational compensation survey. Selected metropolitan areas.* BLS. L 2.121/54:yr. annual.

Summarizes occupational earnings data for the 61 metropolitan areas surveyed during the year as well as establishment practices and benefits for 30 of these areas. For more detailed statistics on these metro-politan areas, see *Occupational compensation survey.* (VIII.11).

VIII.13.*Occupational compensation survey. Summary.* BLS. L 2.122/no.:no./yr. annual or biennial.

These summary reports present hourly earnings and benefits of selected office and plant workers common to a wide variety of industries. Limited to establishments of 50 or more employees, they cover over 100 labor market areas which include smaller MSAs, other metro areas, and other selected labor market areas not included in the series cited above (VIII.11). The occupational coverage is similar to the other series but less detailed. As with the other series, they are given an alphanumeric classification, alphabetically by state, then alphabetically by metropolitan area within each state. They are listed here alphabetically by metropolitan area or other labor market area. Previously published under the title *Area wage survey. Summary.*

Alaska. L 2.122/2:yr.

Albany, GA L 2.122/10:Al 1/yr.

Albany-Schenectady-Troy, NY L 2.122/32:Al l/yr.

Albuquerque, NM L 2.122/31:Al l/yr.

Alexandria-Leesville, LA L 2.122/18:Al 2/yr.

Alpena-Standish-Tawas City, MI. L 2.122/22:Al 7/yr.

Ann Arbor, MI L 2.122/22:An 7/yr.

Asheville, NC L 2.122/33:As 3/yr.

Atlantic City, NJ L 2.122/30:At 6/yr.

Austin, TX L 2.122/43:Au 7/yr.

Bakersfield, CA L 2.122/5:B 17/yr.

Baton Rouge, LA L 2.122/18:B 32/yr.

Battle Creek, MI L 2.122/22:B 32/yr.

Beaumont-Port Arthur-Orange and Lake Charles, TX-LA L 2.122/43:B 38/yr.

Biloxi-Gulfport and Pascagoula, MS L 2.122/24:B 49/r

Binghamton, NY L 2.122/32:B 51/yr.

Birmingham, AL L 2.122/1:B 53/yr.

Bloomington-Vincennes, IN L 2.122/14:B 62/yr.

Bremerton-Shelton, WA L 2.122/47:B 75/yr.

Brunswick, GA L 2.122/10:B 83/yr.

Cedar Rapids, IA L 2.122/15:C 32/yr.

Champaign-Urbana-Rantoul, IL L 2.122/13:C 35/yr.

Charleston, SC L 2.122/40:C 38/yr.

Charlotte-Gastonia-Rockhill, NC-SC L 2.122/33:C 37/yr.

Chattanooga, TN-GA L 2.122/39:C 39/yr.

Cheyenne, WY L 2.122/50:C 42/yr.

Clarksville-Hopkinsville, TN-KY L 2.122/42:C 56/yr.

Columbia-Sumter, SC L 2.122/40:C 72/yr.

Columbus, GA.-AL L 2.122/10:C 72/yr.

Columbus, MS L 2.122/24:C 72/yr.

Connecticut. L 2.122/7:C 76/yr.

Dayton-Springfield, OH L 2.122/35:D 35/yr.

Daytona Beach, FL L 2.122/9:D 33/yr.

Decatur, IL L 2.122/13:D 35/yr.

Des Moines, IA L 2.122/15:D 45/yr,

Dothan, AL L 2.122/1:D 74/yr.

Duluth, MN-WI L 2.122/23:D 88/yr.

El Paso-Alamogordo-Las Cruces, TX-NM
     L 2.122/43:El l/yr.

Eugene-Springfield-Medford-Roseburg-Klamath Falls-
     Grants Pass, OR L 2.122/37:Eu 4/yr.

Fayetteville, NC L 2.122/33:F 29/yr.

Fort Lauderdale-Hollywood-Pompano Beach, FL
     L 2.122/9:F 77/yr.

Fort Smith, AR-OK L 2.122/4:F 77s/yr.

Fort Wayne, IN L 2.122/14:F 77/yr.

Gadsden and Anniston, AL L 2.122/1:G 11/yr.

Goldsboro, NC L 2.122/33:G 57/yr.

Grand Island-Hastings, NE L 2.122/27:G 76/yr.

Green Bay, WI L 2.122/49:G 82/yr.

Greensboro-Winston Salem-High Point, NC
    L 2.122/33:G 85/yr.

Greenville-Spartanburg, SC. L 2.122/40:G 85/yr.

Hagerstown-Cumberland-Chambersburg, MD-PA-WV
    L 2.122/20:H 12/yr.

Harrisburg-Lebanon, PA L 2.122/38:H 24/yr.

Jacksonville, FL L 2.122/9:J 31/yr.

Jacksonville-New Bern, NC L 2.122/33:J 13/yr.

Knoxville, TN L 2.122/42:K 77/yr.

La Crosse-Sparta, WI L 2.122/49:L 11/yr.

Laredo, TX L 2.122/43:L 32/yr.

Las Vegas-Tenopah, NV L 2.122/28:L 33v/yr.

Lexington-Fayette, KY L 2.122/17:L 59/yr.

Lima, OH L 2.122/35:L 62/yr.

Logansport-Peru, IN L 2.122/14:L 82/yr.

Lorain-Elyria, OH L 2.122/35:L 88/yr.

Lower Eastern Shore, MD-VA-DE L 2.122/20:L 95/yr.

Macon-Warner Robins, GA L 2.122/10:M 23/yr.

Madison, WI L 2.122/49:M 26/yr.

Maine. L 2.122/19:M 28/yr.

Manhattan-Junction City, KS L 2.122/16:M 31/yr.

Mansfield, OH L 2.122/35:M 31/2/yr.

McAllen-Edinburg-Mission and Brownsville, TX
    L 2.122/43:M 11/yr.

Melbourne-Titusville-Palm Bay, FL L 2.122/9:M 48/yr.

Meridian, MS L 2.122/24:M 54/yr.

Mobile, AL L 2.122/1:M 71/yr.

Montana. L 2.122/26:M 76/yr.

Montgomery, AL L 2.122/1:M 76/yr.

Norfolk-Virginia Beach-Newport News, VA
    L 2.122/46:N 76/yr.

North Dakota L 2.122/34:N 81d/yr.

Northern New York L 2.122/32:N 42 y/yr.

Northwest Texas L 2.122/43:N 81/yr.

Northwestern Florida L 2.122/9:N 81/yr.

Oklahoma City, OK L 2.122/36:Ok 4/yr.

Orlando, FL L 2.122/9:Or 5/yr.

Oxnard-Ventura, CA L 2.122/5:Ox 5/yr.

Peoria, IL L 2.122/13:P 39/yr

Pine Bluff, AR L 2.122/3:P 65/yr.

Portsmouth-Chillicothe-Gallipolis, OH
    L 2.122/35:P 84/yr

Poughkeepsie-Orange County-Kingston, NY
    L 1.122/21:P 86/yr.

Providence, RI L 2.122/39:P 94/yr.

Pueblo, CO L 2.122/6:P 96/yr.

Puerto Rico L 2.122/53:P 96/yr.

Raleigh-Durham, NC L 2.122/33:R 13/yr.

Reno, NV L 2.122/28:R 29/yr.

Saginaw-Bay City-Midland, MI L 2.122/22:Sa l/yr.

Salina, KS L 2.122/16:Sa 3/yr.

Salinas-Seaside-Monterey, CA L 2.122/5:Sa 3/yr.

Sandusky, OH L 2.122/35:Sa 5/yr.

Santa Barbara-Santa Maria-Lompoc, CA
    L 2.122/5:Sa 5b/yr

Savannah, GA L 2.122/10:Sa 9/yr.

Selma, AL L 2.122/1:Se 4/yr.

Shreveport, LA L 2.122/18:Sh 8/yr.yr.

South Dakota L 2.122/41:So 8d/yr.

Southeastern Massachusetts L 2.122/21:So 8/yr.

Southwest Virginia L 2.122/46:So 8/yr.

Spokane, Wash L 2.122/47:Sp 6/yr.

Springfield, IL L 2.122/13:Sp 8/yr.

Stockton, CA L 2.122/5:St 6/yr.

Tacoma, WA L 2.122/47:T 11/yr.

Topeka, KS L 2.122/16:T 62/yr.

Tucson-Douglas, AZ L 2.122/3:T 79/yr.

Tulsa, OK L 2.122/36:T 82/yr.

Upper Peninsula, MI L 2.122/22:Up 6/yr.

Vallejo-Fairfield-Napa, CA L 2.122/5:V 24/yr.

Vermont L 2.122/45:V 59/yr.

Virgin Islands of the U.S. L 2.122/53:V 81/yr.

Waterloo-Cedar Falls, IA L 2.122/15:W 29/yr.

West Virginia L 2.122/48:W 52v/yr.

Western Massachusetts L 2.122/21:W 52/yr.

Wichita, KS L 2.122/16:W 63/yr.

Wilmington, DE-NJ-MD L 2.122/8:yr.

Yakima-Richland-Kennewick-Pasco-Walla Walla-Pendleton,
    WA-OR L 2.122/47:Y 1/yr.

VIII.14. *U.S. industrial outlook; prospects for 350 industries with 450 tables amd charts.* C 61.34:yr. annual.
Contains industry-by-industry analyses including historical data, current trends, forecasts of future prospects, international competitiveness, and industry statistical profiles. Analyses of each industry gives data for the past five years including employment, number of production workers where applicable, and their average hourly earnings. *U.S. industrial outlook* also included in the CD-*ROM National trade data bank (NTDB).* C 1.88:yr./mo./CD. monthly.

VIII.15. *Occupational outlook handbook.* BLS. L 2.3/4:yr. biennial.
Provides detailed information on about 225 occupa-tions. Occupations that require lengthy education or training are given the most attention. Includes salaries and job outlook for each occupation. *Occupational outlook handbook* also available on CD-ROM: L 2.3/4-4:yr.CD.

VIII.16. *BEA regional projections to 2040.* Commerce Dept., Bureau of Economic Analysis. C 59.17:yr./v.1-3. 3 v. quinquennial.
Presents projections to 2040 of economic activity and population for the nation and the states, metropolitan statistical areas, and BEA economic areas. Vol. 1: *States.* Presents projections for the nation and the states. Provides projections for population in three age groups, personal income, and employment and earnings, each of which is presented for 57 industrial groups. Shows projections for 1995 through 2040 and gives historical data for 1973 through 1988. Vol. 2: *Metropolitan statistical areas.* Presents projections for metropolitan areas for employment by industry and earnings for 1995 through 2040. Vol. 3: *BEA economic areas.* Presents projections of economic activity and population projections for Bureau of Economic Analysis economic areas and the nation.

Private Sector—Nonmanufacturing—Specific Industry

Most of the reports on specific nonmanufacturing industries form part of the *Industry wage survey* series issued by the Bureau of Labor Statistics that covers occupational earnings and employment in specific nonmanufacturing industries. They are all periodically updated, usually every three to five years, or more, depending on the subject. While employment statistics are given in these publications, the statistics are limited to the size of the establishments and not necessarily to all employees in a specific industry. There are also additional wage reports for selected industries covering metropolitan areas and regions.

For documents dealing primarily with manufacturing, *see* Private Sector—Manufacturing p. 124

Agriculture

VIII.17.*Agricultural statistics*. Agriculture Dept. A 1.47:yr. annual.
    A reference book on agricultural production, supplies, consumption, facilities, costs, and returns. Consists of tables of annual data covering commonly used agricultural facts including employment and wages of agricultural workers in the U.S. and regions.

VIII.18.*Residents of farms and rural areas. Current population reports. Series P 20, no. Population characteristics*. Census Bureau. C 3.186:P-20/no. annual.
    Presents a statistical portrait of the farm resident and rural populations of the United States. Information is primarily from the Current Population Survey (CPS).[1] Includes section on "Labor force participation" which gives income and poverty status of farm and nonfarm residents. Previously published under the title *Rural and farm population*.

Airlines

VIII.19.*Industry wage survey. Certified air carriers.* BLS.
L 2.3/3:C 33/yr. irreg.
Summarizes the results of an occupational survey of wages
and related benefits in certified air passenger carriers for
airlines employing 100 workers or more. Data include
earnings of selected occupations in the U.S. airlines.
Description based on survey report of 1989.

Automobile Repair

VIII.20.*Industry wage survey. Auto dealer repair shops.* BLS.
L 2.3/3:Au 8/yr. irreg.
Summarizes the results of a wages and employment benefits
survey in auto dealer repair shops in establishments
employing 20 workers or more in selling new, or new and
used automobiles. Establishments primarily selling trucks and
used cars and general automobile repair shops are not
included. Description based on the survey report of 1988.

Banks and Banking

VIII.21.*Industry wage survey. Banking.* BLS. L 2.3/22:yr. irreg.
Summarizes the results of a survey of occupational wages
and employee benefits in the banking industry for
establishments employing 20 workers or more. Data include
earnings in selected occupations in 19 metropolitan areas.
Description based on the survey report of 1989.

Cleaning Services

VIII.22.*Industry wage survey. Contract cleaning services.* BLS.
L 2.3/33:yr. irreg.
Summarizes the results of an occupational survey of wages
and related benefits in the contract cleaning services
industries for establishments employing eight workers or
more. Data include earnings in selected occupations in 26
metropolitan areas. Description based on survey report of
1986.

Coal Mining

VIII.23.*Industry wage survey. Bituminous coal mining*. BLS.
L 2.3/3:B 54/yr. irreg.
Summarizes the results of an occupational survey of wages
and related benefits in the bituminous coal industry for
establishments employing ten workers or more. Data include
earnings of selected occupations for the U.S., six states
(Alabama, Illinois, Kentucky, E. Kentucky, W. Kentucky,
Pennsylvania, Virginia, W. Virginia) and mountain states.
Description based on the survey report of 1988.

Computer Processing Services

VIII.24.*Industry wage survey. Computer data and processing
services*. BLS. L 2.3/3:C 73/yr. irreg.
Summarizes the results of a survey of occupational wages
and employee benefits in the computer and data processing
services industry for establishments employing eight workers
or more. Data include earnings of selected occupations by sex
for 18 metropolitan areas. Description based on the survey
report of 1987.

Construction

VIII.25.*Construction review*. Commerce Dept., Industry and Trade
Administration. C 61.37:yr. quarterly.
Brings together under one cover virtually all of the
government's current statistics that pertain to construction.
Each issue contains the section "Contract construction
employment," which includes data on gross hours and
earnings of construction workers by type of contractor.

Criminal Justice

VIII.26.*Sourcebook of criminal justice statistics*. Justice Dept.,
Bureau of Justice Statistics. J 29.9/6/yr. annual.
Brings together in a single volume nationwide data of interest
to the criminal justice community. The scope of the data is

national but includes considerable data on regions, states, counties, and cities. Gives salary levels for officers and other employees in the justice system for U.S., states, and combined counties and cities within each state.

Department Stores

VIII.27.*Industry wage survey. Department stores.* BLS. L   2.3/37: yr. irreg.

Summarizes the results of an occupational survey of wages and related benefits of department store employees in regular store establishments employing 100 workers or more, and discount store establish-ments employing 25 workers or more. Data include earnings for occupations in regular stores in 20 metropolitan areas and in discount stores in four metropolitan areas. Description based on the survey report of 1986.

Education

VIII.28.*Condition of education.* National Center for Education Statistics. ED 1.109:yr./v.1-2. annual.

This two-volume set presents detailed data on the current condition of education in the U.S. Volume 1, *Elementary and secondary education,* includes tables on ratio of median annual earnings of young adults (25-34) by years of school completed. Other tables cover average annual and beginning salaries of teachers in public schools by sex, race, and Hispanic origin. Volume 2, *Post secondary education,* includes tables on median starting salaries of college graduates by field of study and average earnings of faculty by field of teaching.

VIII.29.*Digest of education statistics.* National Center for Education Statistics.ED1.310/2:yr./v.1-2.annual..

Provides a compilation of statistical information covering the broad field of American education from kindergarten through graduate school. Includes minimum and average salary of public and private elementary school teachers by state. The same data is given for faculty in higher education institutions. Also includes tables on income of U.S. labor force by years of school completed. *Digest of education statistics* is also included in the CD-ROM *National economic, social, and environmental data book (NESE DB)*. C 1.88/2:yr./no. quarterly.

VIII.30. *Salaries of full-time instructional faculty on 9- and 10-month contracts in institutions of higher education*. National Center for Education Statistics. ED 1.328/3: H 53/2. annual. Covers average salaries of full-time teaching faculty at public and private two-four year institutions of higher education by state. Data are given for current year with trends of the last ten years.

VIII.31. *State higher education profiles, a comparison of state higher education data*. National Center for Education Statistics. ED 1.116/3:yr. annual.
Survey on higher education enrollment, faculty, finances, and degrees in each state and the District of Columbia. Gives nationwide profile on average salary and number of full-time faculty by length of contract and academic rank. For states, gives average salary of all full-time faculty on nine-month contracts.

VIII.32. *State profiles of public elementary and secondary education*. National Center for Education Statistics.
ED 1.328:El 2/yr. biennial.
Gives public education profile for the U.S., each state, and five outlying areas. Each profile includes federal aid to education, enrollment by race and Hispanic origin, and total education staff. States are ranked in "Ranking of states" tables by number of teachers, administrators, average teacher salary, and other comparative data.

Electric Industry

VIII.33. *Industry wage survey. Electric and gas utilities*. BLS. L 2.3/3:El 2/yr. irreg.

Summarizes the results of a survey of occupational wages and employee benefits in privately operated electric and gas utility systems for establishments employing 100 workers or more. Data include wages for selected occupations by sex in the U.S. and nine regions. Description based on the survey report of 1988. Separate reports are available for the following regions:

a. *Electric and gas utilities. Border States Region.*
   L 2.3/3-2:El 2/Border/yr.
b. *Electric and gas utilities. Mountain States Region.*
   L 2.3/3-2:El 2/Mount./yr.
c. *Electric and gas utilities. Pacific Region.*
   L 2.3/3-2:El 2/Pacific/yr.
d. *Electric and gas utilities. Southwest Region.*
   L 2.3/3-2:El 2/South./yr.

Gas Industry

VIII.34.*Industry wage survey. Oil and gas extraction.* BLS. L 2.3/3:Oi 5/yr. irreg.

Summarizes the results of an occupational survey of wages and related benefits in the oil and gas extraction industries for establishments employing eight workers or more in oil and gas field properties, and 20 workers or more in contract drilling. Data include earnings of selected occupations for the U.S., five regions, and five states. Description based on the survey report of 1988.

Health Care

VIII.35.*Health care financing review.* Health and Human Services Dept., Health Care Financing Administration. HE 22.18.v./nos. quarterly with annual supplement.

Contains articles relating to health care financing. Each issue has the table "Health care indicators," which includes employment and earnings for private health service establishments by type of establishment for the current and previous three quarters, and annually for the past three years.

Hospitals

VIII.36.*Industry wage survey. Hospitals.* BLS. L 2.3/3:H 79/ 3/yr.
irreg.
Summarizes the results of a survey of wages in private
hospitals employing 50 workers or more. Data include
earnings of selected occupations for the U.S. and 19
metropolitan areas. Description based on the survey report of
1991. The previous industry wage survey of *Hospitals*, 1989,
covered wages as well as employee benefits.

Hotels

VIII.37.*Industry wage survey. Hotels and motels.* BLS. L 2.3/3:
H 79/2/yr. irreg.
Summarizes the results of an occupational survey of wages
and related benefits of hotel and motel employees in
establishments employing 20 workers or more. Data include
earnings in selected occupations by sex in 18 metropolitan
areas. Separate tabulations given for tipped and nontipped
occupations. Description based on the survey report of 1988.
Separately published reports available for the following
cities:

a. *Hotels and motels. Atlanta, GA*
   L 2.3/3-2:H 79/Atlan./yr.

b. *Hotels and motels. Boston, MA*
   L 2.3/3-2:H 79/Boston/yr.

c. *Hotels and motels. Chicago, IL*
   L 2.3/3-2:H 79/Chica./yr.

d. *Hotels and motels. Dallas, TX*
   L 2.3/3-2:H 79/Dallas/yr.

e. *Hotels and motels. Denver, CO*
   L 2.3/3-2:H 79/Denver/yr.

f. *Hotels and motels. Houston, TX*
   L 2.3/3-2:H 79/Houst./yr.

g. *Hotels and motels. Kansas City, MO-KS*
L 2.3/3-2:H 79/Kansas/yr.

h. *Hotels and motels. Los Angeles-Long Beach, CA*
L 2.3/3-2:H 79/Los A./yr.

i. *Hotels and motels. Miami-Hialeah, FL*
L 2.3/3-2:H 79/Miami/yr.

j. *Hotels and motels. New Orleans, LA*
L 2.3/3-2:H 79/New O./yr.

k. *Hotels and motels. New York, NY*
L 2.3/3-2:H 79/New Y./yr.

l. *Hotels and motels. Philadelphia, PA-NJ*
L 2.3/3-2:H 79/Phila./yr.

m. *Hotels and motels. San Francisco, CA*
L 2.3/3-2:H 79/San F./yr.

n. *Hotels and motels. Washington, DC*
L 2.3/3-2:H 79/Wash./yr.

Insurance

VIII.38.*Industry wage survey. Life and health insurance carriers.*
BLS. L 2.3/3:L 62. irreg.
Summarizes the results of an occupational survey of wages and related benefits in life and health insurance industries. Data include earnings of selected occupations (except sales agents) for the U.S., nine regions, and seven MSAs. Description based on survey report of 1986.

Law Enforcement

VIII.39.*Sheriffs' departments; a LEMAS report.* Justice Dept., Office of Justice Programs, Bureau of Justice Statistics. J 29.11:Sh 5/yr. triennial.
This Law Enforcement Management and Administrative Statistics (LEMAS) report surveys a nationally representative sample of sheriffs' departments and provides data on expenditures, employment, salaries, functions, training and

educational requirements, computerization, programs, and policies.

VIII.40.*Profiles of state and local law enforcement agencies.* Justice Dept., Bureau of Justice Programs, Bureau of Justice Statistics. J 29.11:P 94/yr. irreg.

Contains data on state and local police departments from the Law Enforcement Management and Administrative Statistics (LEMAS) survey. Includes information on operation, equipment, personnel (employment and salaries), and educational and training requirements. Title varies.

Mineral Industry

VIII.41.*Minerals yearbook.* Mines Bureau. I 28.37:yr. 3 v. annual. This three-volume set discusses the annual performance of the worldwide minerals industry. Vol. 1, *Area reports: domestic,* contains chapters on the mineral industry of each of the 50 states, Puerto Rico, Northern Marianas, island possessions, and trust territory. Includes data on employment and wages in mining for most states, especially those with sizable mineral resources.

Nursing Homes

VIII.42.*Industry wage survey. Nursing and personal care facilities.* BLS. L 2.3/25:yr. irreg.

Summarizes the results of a survey of occupational earnings and employee benefits in nursing and personal care facilities employing 20 workers or more. Data include earnings in selected occupations for professional employees, and earnings by sex for nonprofessional occupations, for 22 metropolitan areas. Description based on the survey report of 1985.

Repairing Trade

VIII.43.*Industry wage survey. Appliance repair.* BLS. L 2.3/3:2177. irreg.

Summarizes the results of a wages and employment benefits

Summarizes the results of a wages and employment benefits survey in the TV-radio and electrical appliance repair facilities. Data are tabulated separately for each industry for 19 MSAs. Description based on the survey report of 1981.

Science and Technology

VIII.44. *Characteristics of doctoral scientists and engineers in the U.S.* National Science Foundation. NS 1.22:D 65/yr. biennial.

Presents data on the demographic, social and economic characteristics of the nation's doctoral scientists and engineers. Data include median annual salaries by age, sex, race, and Hispanic origin, by employment sector and primary work activity.

VIII.45. *Science and engineering indicators.* National Science Foundation, National Science Board. NS 1.28/2:yr. biennial.

Overview of developments in science and engineering including education, workforce, and research and development. Earnings cover annual average salary for doctoral and nondoctoral engineers and scientists, and median annual salaries of engineers by industry. Other tables cover salaries for engineers and scientists as well as for other professions.

VIII.46. *Women and minorities in science and engineering.* National Science Foundation. NS 1.49:yr. biennial.

Presents information on the participation of women, racial/ethnic groups (white, African-American, Asian, Native American, and Hispanic), and physically disabled in science and engineering. Covers data for fields of physical sciences, environmental sciences, life sciences, engineering, and various subfields. Gives average salaries by field, sex, and racial/ethnic group.

Service Industries

VIII.47. *White-collar pay: private service-producing industries.* BLS. L 2.3:2347. biennial.

Summarizes the results of the Bureau's biennial survey (in odd-numbered years) of white-collar pay in private service-producing industries, which include transportation, communications, and utilities; finance, insurance, and real estate; wholesale trade; retail trade; and services. Surveys for goods-producing industries (VIII.52) are in even-numbered years. Data collected from establishments employing 50 workers or more. Salaries are divided into four occupational groups: professional, administrative, technical, and clerical, with breakdowns within each group. Description based on the survey of 1989. Previously published under the title *National survey of professional, administrative, technical and clerical pay, private service industries.*

Temporary Employment

VIII.48. *Industry wage survey. Temporary help supply.* BLS. L 2.3/38:yr. irreg.

Summarizes the results of an occupational and wages benefits survey in the temporary help supply industry for establishments employing 50 workers or more. Data include earnings for temporary and permanent workers for selected occupations in 26 metropolitan areas. Description based on the survey report of 1987. Separately published reports are available for the following cities:

a. *Temporary help supply. Anaheim-Santa Ana, CA*
   L 2.3/3-2:T 24/Anahe./yr.

b. *Temporary help supply. Atlanta, GA*
   L 2.3/3-2:T 24/Atlan./yr.

c. *Temporary help supply. Baltimore, MD*
   L 2.3/3-2:T 24/Baltim./yr.

d. *Temporary help supply. Bergen-Passaic, NJ*
   L 2.3/3-2:T 24/Bergen/yr.

e. *Temporary help supply. Boston, MA*
   L 2.3/3-2:T 24/Boston/yr.

f. *Temporary help supply. Chicago, IL*
   L 2.3/3-2:T 24/Chica./yr.

g. *Temporary help supply. Cincinnati, OH-KY-IN*
   L 2.3/3-2:T 24/Cincin./yr.

h. *Temporary help supply. Dallas, TX*
   L 2.3/3-2:T 24/Dallas/yr.

i. *Temporary help supply. Denver, CO*
   L 2.3/3-2:T 24/Denver/yr.

j. *Temporary help supply. Detroit, MI*
   L 2.3/3-2:T 24/Detroit/yr.

k. *Temporary help supply. Fort Lauderdale-Hollywood-*
   Pompano Beach, FL L 2.3/3-2:T 24/Fort L./yr.

l. *Temporary help supply. Houston, TX*
   L 2.3/3-2:T 24/Houst./yr.

m. *Temporary help supply. Indianapolis, IN*
   L 2.3/3-2:T 24/Indian./yr.

n. *Temporary help supply. Kansas City, MO-KS*
   L 2.3/3-2:T 24/Kansas/yr.

o. *Temporary help supply. Los Angeles-Long Beach, CA*
   L 2.3/3-2:T 24/Los A./yr.

p. *Temporary help supply. Minneapolis-St. Paul, MN-WI.*
   L 2.3/3-2:T 24/Minn./yr.

q. *Temporary help supply. New York, NY*
   L 2.3/3-2:T 24/New Y./yr.

r. *Temporary help supply. Newark, NJ*
   L 2.3/3-2:T 24/Newark/yr.

s. *Temporary help supply. Philadelphia, PA-NJ*
   L 2.3/3-2:T 24/Phila./yr.

t. *Temporary help supply. Portland, OR*
   L 2.3/3-2:T 24/Port./yr.

u. *Temporary help supply. San Antonio, TX*
L 2.3/3-2:T 24/San A./yr.

v. *Temporary help supply. San Diego, CA*
L 2.3/3-2:T 24/San D./yr.

w. *Temporary help supply. San Francisco, CA*
L 2.3/3-2:T 24/San F./yr.

x. *Temporary help supply. San Jose, CA*
L 2.3/3-2:T 24/San J./yr.

y. *Temporary help supply. Seattle, WA*
L 2.3/3-2:T 24/Seat./yr.

z. *Temporary help supply. Washington, DC-MD-VA*
L 2.3/3-2:T 24/Wash./yr.

Transportation

VIII.49.*National transportation statistics: annual report.* Transportation Dept., Research and Special Programs Administration. TD 10.9:yr. annual.
Summarizes selected transportation statistics from a wide variety of government and private sources. Includes data on employment and earnings in major sectors of transportation and of related industries for the past ten years.

Private Sector—Manufacturing

VIII.50.*Hourly compensation costs for production workers in manufacturing.* BLS, Productivity and Technology Office. L 2.2:C 73/8/yr. irreg., approximately twice a year.
This series of reports covers costs for production workers for 40 manufacturing industries in the U.S. and 32 foreign countries. Title and content vary slightly with each issue.

VIII.51.*International comparisons of hourly compensation costs for production workers in manufacturing.* BLS. L 2.130:yr. semiannual.
Presents highlights of comparative levels and trends in hourly compensation costs for production workers in manufacturing

in 30 countries or areas. Costs are given for current year and for selective years back to 1975. Besides wages, costs include expenditures for insurance programs and contractual and private benefit plans.

VIII.52. *White-collar pay: private goods-producing industries.* BLS. L 2.3:2374. biennial.

Summarizes the results of the Bureau's survey in even numbered years of white-collar pay in private goods-producing industries, which include manufacturing, construction, and mining. Surveys for service-producing industries (VIII.47) are in odd-numbered years. Data was collected from establishments employing 50 workers or more. Salaries are divided into four occupational categories: professional, administrative, technical, and clerical, with breakdowns within each category. Description based on the survey of 1990. Previously published under the title *National survey of professional, administrative, technical and clerical pay: private nonservice industries.*

Private Sector—Manufacturing—Specific industry

As with nonmanufacturing industries, most of the reports on specific manufacturing industries form part of the *Industry wage survey* series issued by the Bureau of Labor Statistics that covers occupational earnings and employment in specific manufacturing industries. They are all updated periodically, usually every three to five years, or more, depending on the subject. While employment statistics are given in these publications, the statistics are limited to size of establishments, and not necessarily to all employees in a specific industry. There are also additional wage reports for selected industries covering specific metropolitan areas and regions.

Automobile Industry

VIII.53. *Industry wage survey. Motor vehicles and parts.* BLS. L 2.3/3:M 85/yr. irreg.

Summarizes the results of a survey of occupational wages

and related benefits in the motor vehicles and parts industry. Data include employment and earnings for the motor vehicle industry for the U.S., three regions, and Michigan; and for the parts industry for the U.S., four regions and four labor market areas. Description based on the survey report of 1989.

Chemical Industry

VIII.54. *Industry wage survey. Industrial chemicals.* BLS. L 2.3/31:yr. irreg.
Summarizes the results of a survey of wages and employee benefits in industrial chemicals for establishments employing 50 workers or more. Data covers selected occupations for the U.S. and nine regions. Description based on the survey report of 1986.

Cigarette Industry

VIII.55. *Industry wage survey. Cigarette manufacturing.* BLS. L 2.3/26:yr. irreg.
Summarizes the results of a survey of employee wages and benefits in the cigarette manufacturing industry. Survey covers earnings for selected occupations in establishments having 50 or more workers. Description based on the survey report of 1986.

Clay Industries

VIII.56. *Industry wage survey. Structural clay products.* BLS. L 2.3/30:yr. irreg.
Summarizes the results of a survey of wages and related benefits in the structural clay products industries for establishments employing 20 workers or more. Data include selected occupations for the U.S. and seven regions: Mid Atlantic, Border States, Southeast, Southwest, Great Lakes, Mid West, and Pacific. Description based on survey report of 1986.

Clothing

VIII.57.*Industry wage survey. Men's and boys' shirts.* BLS.
L 2.3/3:M 32/3/yr. irreg.
Summarizes the results of a survey of occupational earnings
and employee benefits in the men's and boys' shirts industry
for establishments with 20 or more workers. Data covers
selected occupations by sex for the U.S. and selected regions,
states, and localities. Description based on the survey report
of 1990.

VIII.58.*Industry wage survey. Men's and boys' suits and coats.* BLS.
L 2.3/3:M 52/2/yr. irreg.
Summarizes the results of a survey of occupational wages
and related benefits in the men's and boys' suit and coat
manufacturing industry for establishments employing five
workers or more. Data covers selected occupations by sex for
the U.S. and selected occupations for six regions: Northeast,
Middle Atlantic, Border States, Southeast, Southwest, and
Great Lakes. Description based on the survey report of 1989.

VIII.59.*Industry wage survey. Women's and misses' dresses.* BLS.
L 2.3/3:no. irreg.
Summarizes the results of a survey of wages and related
benefits in the women's and misses' dress manufacturing
industry for establishments employing eight workers or more.
Data include earnings for selected occupations by sex for
selected states and metropolitan areas. Description based on
survey report of 1982.

Flour Mills

VIII.60.*Industry wage survey. Grain mill products.* BLS. L 2.3/3:G
76/yr. irreg.
Summarizes the results of a survey of occupational earnings
and employee benefits in grain mill products industries
covering establishments employing 20 or more workers. Data
covers selected occupations by sex for the U.S. and eight
regions. Description based on the survey report of 1987.

Separately published reports are available for the following regions:

  a. *Flour and other grain mill products. Great Lakes Region.*
     L 2.3/3-2:F 66/Lakes/yr.

  b. *Flour and other grain mill products. Middle West Region.*
     L 2.3/3-2:F 66/Middle/yr.

Furniture Industry

VIII.61.*Industry wage survey. Wood household furniture.* BLS.
    L 2.3/27:yr. irreg.
    Summarizes the results of a survey of occupational earnings
    and employee benefits in the upholstered and nonupholstered
    wood household furniture industries for establishments
    employing 100 workers or more. Data include selected
    occupations by sex for the U.S. and selected regions, states,
    and localities. Description based on the survey report of
    1986.

Glass Manufacture

VIII.62.*Industry wage survey. Pressed or blown glass and
    glassware.* BLS. L 2.3/29:yr. irreg.
    Summarizes the results of an occupational wage and
    employee benefits survey in the pressed or blown glass and
    glassware industries for establishments employing 50 workers
    or more, and for establishments employing 100 workers or
    more in the glass containers industry. Data cover selected
    occupations by sex for the U.S. and six regions: Mid-
    Atlantic, Border States, Southeast, Southwest, Great Lakes,
    and Pacific. Description based on the survey report of 1988.

Hosiery

VIII.63.*Industry wage survey. Hosiery.* BLS. L 2.3/3:H 79/yr. irreg.
    Summarizes the results of a survey of occupational wages
    and employee benefits in the hosiery manufacturing industry

by sex and occupation. Selected from establishments employing 50 workers or more in women's hosiery, and 20 workers or more in hosiery except women's. Description based on survey report of 1987. Separate reports are available for the following regions:

a. *Women's hosiery. Greensboro, Winston-Salem, Highpoint, NC.* L 2.3/3-2:W 84/Green./yr

b. *Women's hosiery, North Carolina.* L 2.3/3-2:W 84/North C./yr.

c. *Women's hosiery, Southeast Region.* L 2.3/3-2:W 84/Southe/yr.

Meat Industry

VIII.64. *Industry wage survey. Meat products.* BLS. L 2.3/15:yr. irreg.

Summarizes the results of a survey of occupational wages and related benefits in the meat products industry. Data include earnings for the U.S. and nine regions. Separate tabulations are given for union and nonunion plants. Description based on the survey report of 1984.

Metalworking Machinery

VIII.65. *Industry wage survey. Metalworking machinery manufacturing.* BLS. L 2.3/3:M 56/yr. irreg.

Summarizes the results of a survey of occupational pay and employee benefits in the metalworking machinery manufacturing industry for establishments employing ten workers or more. Data are provided separately for 12 centers of industry (cities or metropolitan areas). This is the first study of this component of the non-electrical machinery manufac-turing industry. Previously, this information was included in the publication *Machinery manufacturing.* Description based on the survey report of 1990.

Millwork Industry

VIII.66.*Industry wage survey. Millwork.* BLS. L 2.3/14:yr. irreg.
Summarizes the results of a survey of occupational wages and related benefits in the millwork industry for establishments employing eight workers or more. Data include earnings for selected occupations by sex for the U.S. and nine regions. Also includes earnings data for selected states. Description based on the survey report of 1984.

Paper Box Industry

VIII.67.*Industry wage survey. Corrugated and solid fiber boxes.* BLS. L 2.3/3:C 81/yr. irreg.
Summarizes the results of a survey of occupational earnings and employee benefits in the corrugated and solid fiber box manufacturing industry for establishments employing 20 or more workers. Data cover selected occupations by sex for the U.S. and nine regions. Description based on the survey report of 1987. Separately published reports are available for the following areas:

a. *Corrugated and solid fiber boxes. Atlanta, GA*
    L 2.3/3-2:C 81/2/Atlan./yr.

b. *Corrugated and solid fiber boxes. Dallas-Fort Worth, TX*
    L 2.3/3-2:C 81/2/Dallas/yr.

c. *Corrugated and solid fiber boxes. Los Angeles-Long Beach, CA*
    L 2.3/3-2:C 81/2/Los A./yr.

d. *Corrugated and solid fiber boxes. Milwaukee, WI*
    L 2.3/3-2:C 81/2/Milwau/yr.

e. *Corrugated and solid fiber boxes. New York, NY*
    L 2.3/3-2:C 81/2/New Y./yr.

f. *Corrugated and solid fiber boxes. Newark, NJ*
    L 2.3/3-2:C 81/2/Newark/yr.

g. *Corrugated and solid fiber boxes. Philadelphia, PA-NJ*
    L 2.3/3-2:C 81/2/Phila./yr.

h. *Corrugated and solid fiber boxes. St. Louis, MO-IL*
L 2.3/3-2:C 81/2/St. Lou./yr.

Paper Industry

VIII.68. *Industry wage survey. Pulp, paper, and paperboard mills.*
BLS. L 2.3/3:P 96/yr. irreg.
Summarizes the results of an occupational survey in pulp,
paper, and paperboard mills for establishments employing
100 workers or more. Data covers selected occupations for
the U.S. and six regions: New England, Mid Atlantic,
Southeast, Southwest, Great Lakes, and Pacific. Description
based on survey report of 1987.

Petroleum

VIII.69. *Industry wage survey. Petroleum refining.* BLS. L 2.3/3:
P 44/yr.irreg.
Summarizes the results of occupational earnings and
employee benefits in the petroleum refining industry for
establishments employing 100 workers or more. Data
include earnings for selected occupations by sex for the U.S.
and eight regions: East Coast, Western Pennsylvania-West
Virginia, Midwest I, Midwest II, Texas-Louisiana Gulf
Coast, Texas Inland-North Louisiana-Arkansas, Rocky
Mountain, and West Coast. Description based on survey
report of 1988.

Shipbuilding Industry

VIII.70. *Report on survey of U.S. shipbuilding and repair facilities.*
Transportation Dept., Maritime Administration. TD 11.25:
yr. annual.
Reports on major shipbuilding, repair, and drydocking
facilities. Includes data on shipyard employment and
earnings.

VIII.71. *Industry wage survey. Shipbuilding and repairing.* BLS.
L 2.3/34:yr. irreg.
Summarizes the results of a survey of occupational wages
and employee benefits in the shipbuilding and repairing

industry for establishments employing 100 workers or more, excluding federal facilities. Data include selected occupations for the U.S. and four areas: Atlantic Coast, Gulf Coast, Great Lakes, and Pacific Coast. Description based on survey report of 1986.

Shoe Industry

VIII.72. *Industry wage survey. Men's and women's footwear.* BLS. L 2.3/3:no. irreg.

Summarizes the results of a survey of occupational wages and related benefits in the men's and women's footwear manufacturing industry. Data include earnings for men's footwear plants for the U.S., seven regions, and five states; and for women's footwear plants for the U.S., three regions, and three states. Description based on the survey report of 1986.

Steel Industry

VIII.73. *Quarterly report on the status of the steel industry. Report to the Committee on Ways and Means on Investigation no. 332-226 under section 332 of the Tariff act of 1930.* International Trade Administration. BLS. ITC 1.27: (date). quarterly.

Provides data on U.S. steel imports by country, and the U.S. steel industry operations and finances, including tables on wages in the steel industry.

VIII.74. *Industry wage survey. Basic iron and steel.* BLS. L 2.3/3:Ir 6/yr. irreg.

Summarizes the results of an occupational wage survey in basic iron and steel mills employing 100 workers or more. Gives data by occupation for the U.S. and for regions: Northeast, South, Midwest, and West. Description based on the survey report of 1988.

VIII.75. *Industry wage survey. Iron and steel foundries.* BLS. L 2.3/32:yr. irreg.

Summarizes the results of a survey of occupational wages and employee benefits in the iron and steel foundry industries for establishments employing 20 workers or more. Data cover selected occupations by sex for the U.S. and nine regions, selected states, and localities. Description based on the survey report of 1986.

Textile Industry

VIII.76.*Industry wage survey. Synthetic fibers*. BLS. L 2.3/21:yr. irreg.
Summarizes survey of wages and employee benefits in the synthetic manufacturing industry for establish-ments employing 20 workers or more. Data include earnings by selected occupation in the southern states excluding Texas. Description based on survey report of 1985.

VIII.77.*Industry wage survey. Textile plants*. BLS. L 2.3:2386. irreg.
Summarizes the results of a survey of occupational wages and employee benefits for cotton and synthetic textile plants employing 100 workers or more, and for wool textile plants employing 50 workers or more. Data include earnings in selected occupations for the U.S. and four regions, selected states and localities. Description based on survey report of 1990. Previously published under the title *Textile mills*. Bulletin 2265.

Part 2

Ready-Reference Guide

Detailed statistics, compendia, digests, etc., on EMPLOYMENT	NATIONAL	Age/sex/race (wh-bl-Hisp)	STATE	Age/sex/race (wh-bl-Hisp)	COUNTY/METRO	Age/sex/race (wh-bl-Hisp)	CITIES, LOCAL AREAS	Age/sex/race (wh-bl-Hisp)	Congressional district	Zip code	Major industry	Detailed industry	Major occupation	Detailed occupation	Foreign countries
Economic indicators. m. I.21	√										√				
Employment and earnings. m. I.1	√	√	√		√						√	√	√	√	
Monthly labor review. m. I.3	√	√	√								√				√
Survey of current business. m. I.22	√										√				
Unemployment in states & local areas. m. II.5			√		√		√								
Employment and wages, annual averages. a. I.4	√		√								√	√			
Foreign labor trends. a. (foreign countries only) I.24	√										√				√
Geographic profile of employment & unemployment a. II.6	√	√	√	√	√	√	√	√			√		√		
Job patterns for minorities & women in priv. indus. a. IV.2	√	√2	√	√2	√	√2					√		√		
Statistical abstract. a. I.5	√	√	√		√						√		√	√	√
Supplement to employment & earnings. a. I.6	√										√	√			
USA counties. a. I.7	√		√		√						√		√		
Business statistics. b. I.26	√										√				
Census tracts. d. I.8					√	√3	√	√3			√		√		
Population & housing characteristics for congressional districts. d. I.9			√	√2	√	√2	√	√2	√		√		√		
Social & econ. characteristics. d. I.12	√	√3	√	√3	√	√3	√	√3			√		√		
Social & econ. characteristics. Metropolitan areas. d. I.13	√				√	√3					√		√		
Social & econ. characteristics. Urbanized areas. d. I.14	√						√	√3			√		√		
Summary social, econ., & housing characteristics. d. I.10	√		√		√		√								
Summary tape file (STF):															
3.A. Summary for states, etc. d. I.11				√		√		√			√		√		
3.B. Zip code areas. d. I.11										√	√		√		
3.C. U.S. summary includes regions, states, etc. d. I.11				√		√		√			√		√		
3.D. Congressional districts. d. I.11				√				√	√		√		√		
County & city data book. irreg. I.15	√		√		√		√				√				
Emplymt., hours & earnings, states, areas, 1987-92 irreg. I.16			√		√						√				
Emplymt., hours & earnings, U.S. 1909-94. irreg. I.17	√										√	√			
Emplymt., hours & earnings, U.S. 1981-93. irreg. I.18	√										√	√			
Handbook of labor statistics. irreg. I.19	√	√	√								√	√	√	√	√
Labor force stats. from Current Pop. Survey. irreg. I.20	√	√									√	√	√	√	
Revised seasonally adjusted labor force statistics, 1978-87. irreg. II.7	√	√									√				
State & metropolitan area data book. irreg. I.27			√		√		√				√				

Notes: 1. Race—white/black only. 2. Excludes age, includes all races & Hispanic.
3. Race—All races & Hispanic.
Frequency of publication: a. annual; b. biennial; d. decennial; irreg. irregular; m. monthly

Detailed statistics, compendia, digests, etc., on UNEMPLOYMENT	NATIONAL	Age/sex/race (wh-bl-Hisp)	STATE	Age/sex/race (wh-bl-Hisp)	COUNTY/METRO	Age/sex/race (wh-bl-Hisp)	CITIES, LOCAL AREAS	Age/sex/race (wh-bl-Hisp)	Congressional district	Zip code	Major industry	Major occupation	Foreign countries
Economic indicators. m. I.21	√	√1											
Employment and earnings. m. I.1	√	√	√		√						√	√	
Employment situation. m. I.2	√										√	√	
Monthly labor review. m. I.3	√	√	√								√		√
Survey of current business. m. I.22	√												
Unemployment in state & local areas. m. II.5				√		√		√					
Employment and wages, annual averages. a. I.4													
Foreign labor trends. a. (foreign countries only) I.24	√												√
Geographic profile of employment & unemployment a. II.6	√	√	√	√	√	√	√	√			√	√	
Job patterns for minorities & women in priv. indus. a. IV.2													
Statistical abstract. a. I.5	√	√	√		√						√	√	√
Supplement to employment & earnings. a. I.6													
USA counties. a. I.7	√			√	√								
Business statistics. b. I.26	√	√									√		
Census tracts. d. I.8					√	√3	√	√3					
Population & housing characteristics for congressional districts. d. I.9			√	√2	√	√2	√	√2	√				
Social & econ. characteristics. d. I.12	√	√3	√	√3	√	√3	√	√3					
Social & econ. characteristics. Metropolitan areas. d. I.13	√				√	√3							
Social & econ. characteristics. Urbanized areas. d. I.14	√						√	√3					
Summary social, econ., & housing characteristics. d. I.10	√		√		√		√						
Summary tape file (STF):													
3.A. Summary for states, etc. d. I.11			√		√		√						
3.B. Zip code areas. d. I.11										√			
3.C. U.S. summary includes regions, states, etc. d. I.11			√		√		√						
3.D. Congressional districts. d. I.11			√		√		√		√				
County & city data book. irreg. I.15	√		√		√		√						
Emplymt., hours & earnings, states, areas, 1987-92 irreg. I.16													
Emplymt., hours & earnings, U.S. 1909-94. irreg. I.17													
Emplymt., hours & earnings, U.S. 1981-93. irreg. I.18													
Handbook of labor statistics. irreg. I.19	√	√	√	√							√	√	√
Labor force stats. from Current Pop. Survey. irreg. I.20	√	√									√	√	
Revised seasonally adjusted labor force statistics, 1978-87. irreg. II.7	√	√									√		
State & metropolitan area data book. irreg. I.27			√		√		√						

Notes: 1. Race—white/black only. 2. Excludes age, includes all races & Hispanic. 3. Race—All races & Hispanic.

Frequency of publication: a. annual; b. biennial; d. decennial; irreg. irregular; m. monthly

Detailed statistics, compendia, digests, etc., on INCOME/EARNINGS	NATIONAL	Age/sex/race (wh-bl-Hisp)	STATE	Age/sex/race (wh-bl-Hisp)	COUNTY/METRO	Age/sex/race (wh-bl-Hisp)	CITIES, LOCAL AREAS	Age/sex/race (wh-bl-Hisp)	Congressional district	Zip code	Major industry	Detailed industry	Major occupation	Detailed occupation	Foreign countries
Economic indicators. m. I.21	√														
Employment and earnings. m. I.1	√	√									√	√			
Employment situation. m. I.2	√										√				
Monthly labor review. m. I.3	√										√				
Survey of current business. m. I.22	√		√												
Employment and wages, annual averages. a. I.4	√		√								√	√			
Foreign labor trends. a. (foreign countries only) I.24	√										√			√	√
Local area personal income. a. VI.3	√		√		√										
Money income & poverty status in the U.S. a. VI.4	√	√													
Money income of households, families, & persons. a. VI.5	√	√													
Regional economic information system. a. VI. 5A			√		√							√			
Statistical abstract. a. I.5	√	√	√		√										
Supplement to employment & earnings. a. I.6	√											√	√		
USA counties. a. I.7	√		√		√										
Business statistics. b. I.26	√										√				
Local pop. estimates. Population & per capita income estimates for countries and incorporated places. b. VI.6	√		√		√		√								
Census tracts. d. I.8					√	√[1,2]	√	√[1,2]							
Population & housing characteristics for congressional districts. d. I.9			√	√[1,2]	√	√[1,2]	√	√[1,2]	√						
Social & econ. characteristics. d. I.12	√	√[1]	√	√[1]	√	√[1]	√	√[1]							
Social & econ. characteristics. Metropolitan areas. d. I.13	√				√	√[1,2]									
Social & econ. characteristics. Urbanized areas. d. I.14	√						√	√[1,2]							
Summary social, econ., & housing characteristics. d. I.10	√		√		√		√								
Summary tape file (STF):															
3.A. Summary for states, etc. d. I.11			√		√		√								
3.B. Zip code areas. d. I.11										√					
3.C. U.S. summary includes regions, states, etc. d. I.11	√		√		√		√								
3.D. Congressional districts. d. I.11			√				√		√						
County & city data book. irreg. I.19	√		√		√		√								
Emplymt., hours & earnings, states, areas, 1987-92 irreg. I.16			√		√						√				
Emplymt., hours & earnings, U.S. 1909-94. irreg. I.17	√										√	√			
Emplymt., hours & earnings, U.S. 1981-93. irreg. I.18	√										√	√			
Handbook of labor statistics. irreg. I.19	√	√	√								√	√	√	√	√
Labor force stats. from Current Pop. Survey. irreg. I.20	√	√[3]									√		√		
State & metropolitan area data book. irreg. I.27	√		√		√		√								
State personal income, 1929- . irreg. VI.8	√		√												
Trends in income, selected characteristics, 1947-88. irreg. VI.9	√	√												√	

Notes: 1. All races & Hispanic. 2. Excludes age. 3. Race— white/black only.
Frequency of publication: a. annual; b. biennial; d. decennial; irreg. irregular; m. monthly

Part 3

Appendices

Abbreviations and Acronyms

AFDC	Aid to Families with Dependent Children
AMA	American Medical Association
ASI	American Statistics Index
BEA	Bureau of Economic Analysis (Commerce Dept.)
BLS	Bureau of Labor Statistics
CD	Congressional District
CD-ROM	Compact Disk-Read Only Memory
CIA	Central Intelligence Agency
CMSA	Consolidated Metropolitan Statistical Area
DOD	Department of Defense
DOE	Department of Energy
EC	European Community
EEOC	Equal Employment Opportunity Commission
EIC	Enterprise Industrial Classification
MCD	Minor Civil Division
MSA	Metropolitan Statistical Area
NASA	National Aeronautics and Space Administration
OASDI	Old Age Survivor and Disability Insurance
OECD	Organization for Economic Cooperation and Development
OPEC	Organization of Petroleum Exporting Countries

OPM	Office of Personnel Management
PMSA	Primary Metropolitan Statistical Area
Pt.	Part
R&D	Research and Development
RRG	Ready-Reference Guide
SAT	Scholastic Aptitude Test
S/E	Science and Engineering
SIC	Standard Industrial Classification
SSI	Supplementary Security Income
STF	Summary Tape File
USPS	U.S. Postal Service
V., Vol.	Volume

* see glossary for definition

Glossary

Block—An area bounded on all sides by visible features such as streets, roads, streams, etc. A block is the smallest geographic tabulation area from the 1990 census.

Block numbering area (BNA)—An area delineated cooperatively by the states and the Census Bureau for grouping and numbering blocks in block-numbered areas where census tracts have not been established.

Census tract—A small, relatively permanent division of a metropolitan statistical area or selected nonmetropolitan counties, delineated for presenting census data. Census tracts are designed to be relatively homogeneous for population characteristics, economic status, and living conditions, and to contain between 2,500 and 8,000 inhabitants.

Congressional district (CD)—Congressional districts are the 435 areas from which persons are elected to the U.S. House of Representatives. Each CD is to be as equal in population to all other CDs in the state as practicable, based on the decennial census counts.

Consolidated metropolitan statistical area (CMSA)—A metropolitan area that has more than one million persons. A CMSA is divided into primary metropolitan statistical areas (PMSAs)—see below.

Metropolitan area (MA)—The general concept of a metropolitan area (MA) is one of a large population nucleus, together with adjacent communities that have a high degree of economic and social integration with that nucleus. Some of the MAs are defined around two or more nuclei. The term "MA" is generic and includes metropolitan statistical areas (MSAs), consolidated metropolitan statistical areas (CMSAs), and primary metropolitan statistical areas (PMSAs) within the qualifying MA.

Metropolitan statistical area (MSA)—A highly populated, economically integrated area defined by the Office of Management and Budget as a federal statistical standard. An area qualifies for recognition as a MSA in one of two ways: it contains a city of at least 50,000 population, or an urbanized area of at least 50,000 with a total metropolitan population of at least 100,000 (75,000 in New England). Metropolitan statistical areas are relatively freestanding MAs and are not closely associated with other MAs.

Minor civil division (MCD)—An MCD is the primary legal or administrative division of a county in 28 states. MCDs are identified by a variety of legal designations such as township, town, borough, magisterial district, or gore.

Primary metropolitan statistical area (PMSA)—PMSAs consist of a large urbanized county or cluster of counties that demostrates very strong internal economic and social links, in addition to close ties to other portions of the larger area. The larger area of which they are component parts is designated a consolidated metropolitan statistical area (CMSA)—see above.

Region—A large grouping of states for presentation of census data.

Urbanized area (UA)—A densely settled area consisting of a central place (or places) and surrounding closely settled territory ("urban fringe") that together have a minimum population of 50,000.

Notes

1. Current Population Survey (CPS), household survey, is a monthly survey of about 60,000 households which provides monthly statistics on employment, unemployment, and related subjects. It is conducted by the Bureau of the Census for the Bureau of Labor Statistics using a scientifically selected sample of households, representative of the civilian noninstitu-tional population of the United States.

2. Current Employment Survey (CES), establishment survey, is a monthly survey based on payroll records of a sample of over 350,000 nonagricultural establishments. It is jointly managed by the individual states and the Bureau of Labor Statistics. Its purpose is to report monthly employment, hours, and earnings information for the nation, the states, and selected local areas within the states.

3. *STF (Summary tape file),* a decennial census release first issued after the 1970 census, provides extensive data on population and housing in far greater subject and geographic detail than that provided by the printed reports.

4. Local Area Unemployment Statistics (LAUS) program, like the CES program, is a federal-state cooperative program in which estimates are prepared by state employment security agencies using concepts, definitions, and estimation procedures prescribed by the BLS.

5. Occupational Employment Survey (OES) is a periodic mail survey conducted by state employment security agencies of a sample of nonfarm establishments to obtain wage and salary employment by occupation. These data are used to estimate total employment by occupation for the nation, for each state, and for selected areas within each state.

6.   AMA physician masterfile is the most comprehensive and complete source of physician data in the United States. It includes information on every physician in the country, on graduates of American medical schools who are temporarily practicing overseas, and graduates of foreign medical schools who are in the United States and meet U.S. education standards for primary recognition as physicians.

7.   Survey of Income and Program Participation (SIPP) is a Census Bureau survey that collects national data on income distribution and poverty. These data are used to study programs, such as Social Security, AFDC, Medicare, and others, to estimate future program costs and coverage, and to assess the effects of proposed changes in program eligibility rules or benefit levels.

Title Index

Affirmative employment statistics. (PM 1.10/2-3:), V.3.

Aging America, trends and projections. (Y 3.F 31/15:2 Ag 4/2), IV.26, VII.22.

Agricultural statistics. (A 1.47:), V.37, VIII.17.

American Indian and Alaska native areas. (Census of population. Social and economic characteristics).
(C 3.223/7-2:990 CP-2-1A/sec.1-2), IV.15, VII.10.

The American workforce: 1992-2005. (L 2.3:2452), III.3.

Ancestry of the population in the United States. (Census of population).
(C 3.223/10:990 CP-3-2), IV.17, VII.12.

Annual report. (U.S. Railroad Retirement Board). (RR 1.1:), V.66.

Annual report of the Postmaster General. (P.1.1:), V.10.

Annual report of the President to the Congress on the operation of the Automotive products trade act of 1965. V.94.

Annual report on the employment of minorities, women and people with disabilities in the federal government. (Y 3.Eq 2:12/5/), V.2, VIII.1.

Annual survey of manufactures. Geographic area statistics. (C 3.24/9-9:), V.84.

Annual survey of manufactures. Statistics for industry groups and industries.
(C 3.24/9-7:), V.85.

Appliance repair. (L 2.3/3:2177), VIII.43.

Asian and Pacific Islander population in the United States.
(C 3.186:P 20/459), IV.11, VII.7.

Asians and Pacific Islanders in the United States. (Census of population).
(C 3.223/10:990 CP-3-5), IV.8, VII.4.

Auto dealer repair shops. (L 2.3/3:Au 8/), VIII.20

Banking. (L 2.3/22:), VIII.21.

Basic iron and steel. (L 2.3/3:Ir 6/), VIII.74.

BEA regional projections to 2040. (C 59.17:), III.6, VIII.16.

Biennial report of employment by geographic area. (PM 1.10/3:), V.4.

Bituminous coal mining. (L 2.3/3:B 54/), VIII.23.

Black news digest. (L 1.20/6:), IV.5, VII.1.

The black population in the United States. (C 3.186:P 20/), IV.6, VII.2.

Bulletin of hardwood market statistics. (A 13.79/3:), V.58.

Business statistics. (C 59.11/3:), I.26.

Career guide to industries. (L 2..3/4-3:), III.2, V.19, VIII.10A.

Census of construction industries. Geographic area series.
    (C 3.245/7:CC 87-A-), V.40.

Census of construction industries. Industry series. (C 3.245/3:CC 92--I-), V.41.

Census of governments. Public employment. (C 3.145/4:v.3), V.15, VIII.9.

Census of manufactures. Geographic area series.
    (C 3.24/3:MC 92-A-), V.90.

Census of manufactures. Industry series. (C 3.24/4:MC 92-I-), V.91.

Census of manufactures. Subject series. General summary.
    (C 3.24/12:MC-[yr.]-S-1), V.92.

Census of mineral industries. Geographic area series.
    (C 3.216/2:MIC 87-A-), V.62.

Census of mineral industries. Industry series.
    (C 3.216:MIC-92-I-), V.63.

Census of mineral industries. Subject series. General summary.
    (C 3.216/4:MIC 87-S-1), V.64.

Census of population. Ancestry of the population in the United States.
    (C 3.223/10:990 CP-3-2), IV.17, VII.12.

Census of population and housing. Equal employment opportunity file.
    (C 3.283:CD 90-EEO-1-2), IV.4, V.35.

Census of population and housing. Population and housing characteristics for census tracts (C 3.223/11:990 CPH-3-), I.8.

Census of population and housing. Population and housing characteristics for congressional districts.
    (C 3.223/20:990-CPH-4-), I.9.

Census of population and housing. Special tabulation on aging.
    (C 3.231/2:CD 90-AOA1), IV.25, VII.21.

Census of population and housing. Summary social, economic, and housing characteristics. (C 3.223/23:990 CPH-5-), I.10.

Census of population and housing. Summary tape file (STF) 3.
    (C 3.282/2:CD 90-3A-), I.11.

Census of population. Asians and Pacific Islanders in the United States.
    (C 3.223/10:990 CP- 3-5), IV.9, VII.4.

Census of population. Characteristics of American Indians by tribe and language.
    (C 3.223/10:990 CP-3-7/sec.1-2), IV.14B, VII.9B.

Census of population. Characteristics of the black population.
    (C 3.223/10:990 CP-3-6), IV.6A, VII.2A.

Census of population. Education in the United States.
    (C 3.223/10:990 CP-3-4), VII.26.

Census of population. The foreign-born population in the United States.
    (C 3.223/10:990 CP-3-1), IV.18, VII.13.

Census of population. Persons of Hispanic origin in the United States. (C 3.223/10:990 CP-3-3), IV.14, VII.9.

Census of population. Social and economic characteristics. (C 3.223/7:990 CP-2-), I.12.

Census of population. Social and economic characteristics. American Indian and Alaska native areas. (C 3.223/7-2:990 CP-2-1A/sec.1-2) , I V.15, VII.10.

Census of population. Social and economic characteristics. Metropolitan areas. (C 3.223/7-3:990 CP-2-1B/sec.1-6), I.13.

Census of population. Social and economic characteristics. Urbanized areas. (C 3.223/7-4:990 CP-2-1C/sec.1-6), I.14.

Census of retail trade. Geographic area series. (C 3.255/2:RC 92-A-), V.67.

Census of service industries. Geographic area series. (C 3.257/2:SC 92-A-), V.75.

Census of transportation. Geographic area series. Selected transportation industries. Summary. (C 3.233/5:TC 87 A-1), V.80.

Census of transportation. Subject series. Selected transportation industries. Miscellaneous subjects. (C 3.233/5:TC 87 S-1), V.81.

Census of wholesale trade. Geographic area series. (C 3.256/2:WC 92 A-), V.82.

Census of wholesale trade. Subject series. Miscellaneous subjects. (C 3.256/3:WC 87-S-4), V.83.

Certified air carriers. (L 2.3/3:C 33), VIII.19.

Characteristics of American Indians by tribe and language. (Census of population). (C 3.223/10:990 CP-3-7/sec.1-2), IV.14B, VII.9B.

Characteristics of doctoral scientists and engineers in the U.S. (NS 1.22:D 65/), V.69, VIII.44.

Characteristics of physicians. (HE 20.6617:), V.65.

Characteristics of the black population. (Census of population). (C 3.223/10:990 CP-3-6), IV.6A, VII.2A..

Chartbook on work disability in the United States. (ED 1.2:D 63/8/), IV.27, VII.23.

Children in custody. (J 32.2:C 43/5/), V.43.

Cigarette manufacturing. (L 2.3/26:), VIII.55.

City employment. (C 3.140/2-3:), V.11, VIII.5.

Coal production. (E 3.11/7-3:), V.59.

Commerce publications update. (C 1.24/3:), II.1.

Company summary. (Enterprise statistics). (C 3.230:ES 87-3), V.33.

Compensation and working conditions. (L 2.44:), VI.1.

Computer data and processing services. (L 2.3/3:C 73/), VIII.24.

Life and health insurance carriers. (L 2.3/3:L 62), VIII.38.

Local area personal income. (C 59.18:), VI.3.

Local population estimates. Population and per capita income estimates for counties and incorporated places: Northeast. (C 3.186/27:); West. (C 3.186/27-2:); West North Central. (C 3.186/27-3:); East North Central. (C 3.186/27-4:); South. (C 3.186/27-5:); VI.6.

Manufacturers shipments to the federal government. (Census of manufactures. Subject series). (C 3.24/12:MC[yr]-S-7), V.92.

Meat products. (L 2.3/15:), VIII.64.

Men's and boys' shirts. (L 2.3/3:M 32/3/), VIII.57.

Men's and boys' suits and coats. (L 2.3/3:M 52/2/), VIII.58.

Men's and women's footwear. (L 2.3/3:), VIII.72.

Metalworking machinery manufacturing. (L 2.3/3:M 56/), VIII.65.

Metropolitan areas. (Census of population. Social and economic characteristics). (C 3.223/7-3:990 CP-2-1B/sec.1-6), I.13.

Military manpower statistics. (D 1.61:), V.6.

Millwork. (L 2.3/14:), VIII.66.

Mineral commodity summaries. (I 28.148:), V.60.

Minerals yearbook. (I 28.37:), V.61, VIII.41.

Minority workers. (L 2.41/11-2:), IV.1.

Miscellaneous subjects. (Census of transportation. Subject series. Selected transportation industries). (C 3.233/5:TC 87 S-1), V.81.

Miscellaneous subjects. (Census of wholesale trade. Subject series). (C 3.256/3:WC 87-S-4), V.83.

Money income and poverty status in the United States. (C 3.186/11:), VI.4.

Money income of households, families, and persons in the United States. (C 3.186/2:), VI.5.

Monthly labor review. (L 2.6:), I.3.

Motor vehicles and parts. (L 2.3/3:M 85/), VIII.53.

National survey of professional, administrative, technical, and clerical pay: private nonservice industries. *see* White-collar pay: private goods-producing industries.

National survey of professional, administrative, technical, and clerical pay: private service industries. *see* White-collar pay: private service-producing industries.

National transportation statistics: annual report. (TD 10.9:), V.79, VIII.49.

News. Employment and wages in foreign-owned businesses in the United States. (L 2.41/12:), V.16, VIII.10.

News. State and metropolitan area employment and unemployment. (L 2.111/5:), II.4.

News. Union members. (L 2.120/2-12:), IV.32, VII.35.

News. Usual weekly earnings of wage and salary workers.
    (L 2.126:), VI.2.

Noticias de la semana: a news summary for Hispanics. (L 1.20/7:), IV.12.

Nursing and personal care facilities. (L 2.3/25:), VIII.42.

OASDI beneficiaries by state and county. (HE 3.73/2:), VII.31.

Occupational compensation survey. (L 2.121/no.:), VIII.11.

Occupational compensation survey. Selected metropolitan areas.
    (L 2.121/54:), VIII.12.

Occupational compensation survey. Summary. (L 2.122/no.:), VIII.13.

Occupational employment in manufacturing industries. (L 2.3/16:), V.88.

Occupational employment in mining, construction, finance, and services.
    (L 2.3:2397), V.26.

Occupational employment in selected nonmanufacturing industries.
    (L 2.3/16-2:), V.27.

Occupational employment in transportation, communications, utilities, and trade.
    (L 2.3:2220), V.36.

Occupational outlook handbook. (L 2.3/4:), III.4, V.24, VIII.15.

Occupational outlook quarterly. (L 2.70/4:), III.1, V.17.

Occupational projections and training data. (L 2.3/4-2:), III.5, V.25.

Occupations of federal white-collar and blue-collar workers.
    (PM 1.10/2-2:), V.5, VIII.4.

Oil and gas extraction. (L 2.3/3:Oi 5/), VIII.34.

Outlook 1990-2005 *see* The American workforce: 1992-2005.

Pay structure of the federal civil service. (PM 1.10/2:P 29/), VIII.2.

Pensions, worker coverage and retirement benefits. (C 3.186:P-70/2/), VII.29.

Persons of Hispanic origin in the United States. (Census of population).
    (C 3.223/10:990 CP-3-3), IV.14, VII.9.

Petroleum refining. (L 2.3/3:P 44/), VIII.69.

Population and housing characteristics for census tracts. (Census of population and
    housing). (C 3.223/11:990 CPH-3-), I.8.

Population and housing characteristics for congressional districts. (Census of
    population and housing). (C 3.223/20:990 CPH-4-), I.9.

Population and per capita income estimates for counties and incorporated places.
    (C 3.186/27--C 3.186/27-5),VI.6.

Population profile of the United States. (C 3.186/8:), I.25.

Poverty in the United States. (C 3.186/22:), VII.28.

President's comprehensive triennial report on immigration. (J 21.21:) IV.29.

Pressed or blown glass and glassware. (L 2.3/29:), VIII.62.

Selected transportation industries. Summary. (Census of transportation. Geographic area series). (C 3.233/5:TC 87 A-1), V.80.

Sheriff's departments; a LEMAS report. (J 29.11:Sh 5/), V.56, VIII.39.

Shipbuilding and repairing. (L 2.3/34:), VIII.71.

Social and economic characteristics. (Census of population).
     (C 3.223/7:990 CP-2-), I.12.

Social and economic characteristics. American Indian and Alaska native areas. (Census of population). C 3.223/7-2: 990 CP-2-1A/sec.1-2), IV.15, VII.10.

Social and economic characteristics. Metropolitan areas. (Census of population). (C 3.223/7-3:990 CP-2-1B/sec.1-6), I.13.

Social and economic characteristics. Urbanized areas. (Census of population). (C 3.223/7-4:990 CP-2-1C/sec.1-6), I.14.

Social security bulletin. (HE 3.3:), VII.30.

Social security bulletin, annual statistical supplement. (HE 3.3/3:), VII.32.

Sourcebook of criminal justice statistics. (J 29.9/6:), V.42, VIII.26.

Special tabulation on aging. (Census of population and housing).
     C 3.281/2:CD 90-AOA1), IV.25, VII.21.>

SSI recipients by state and county. (HE 3.71:), VII.33.

State and metropolitan area data book. (C 3.134/5:), I.27.

State and metropolitan area employment and unemployment. (News).
     (L 2.111/5:), II.4.

State higher education profiles. (ED 1.116/3:), V.48, VIII.31.

The state of small business. (SBA 1.1/2:), V.22.

State personal income. (C 59.2:In 2/4/), VI.8.

State profiles of public elementary and secondary education.
     (ED 1.328:El 2/), V.49, VIII.32.

Statistical abstract of the United States. (C 3.134:), I.5.

Statistics of communications common carriers. (CC 1.35:), V.77.

Statistics for industry groups and industries. (Annual survey of manufactures). (C 3/24/9-7:), V.85.

Structural clay products. (L 2.3/30:), VIII.56.

Subject series. General summary. (Census of manufactures).
     (C 3.24/12:MC[yr.]-S-1), V.92.

Subject series. General summary. (Census of mineral industries).
     (C 3.216/4:MIC 87-S-1), V.64.

Subject Index 1—
Employment/Unemployment

For employment/unemployment covering United States, the invididual states, etc., *see* UNITED STATES; UNITED STATES—CONGRESSIONAL DISTRICTS; UNITED STATES—NATIONAL, STATES; *and other subject subdivisions of* UNITED STATES.

ABILENE, TX, MSA
　　　Census tracts. Report no. 58. decennial. I.8.
AFFIRMATIVE ACTION *see* MINORITIES
AFRICAN-AMERICANS
　　　Black news digest. weekly. IV.5.
　　　The black population of the United States. annual. IV.6.
　　　Census of population. Characteristics of the black population.
　　　　　decennial. IV.6A.
　　　Survey of minority-owned business enterprises. Black. quinquennial.
　　　　　V.29.
　　　We the American...blacks. decennial. IV.7.
AGED
　　　Aging America, trends and projections. irreg. IV.26.
　　　Census of population and housing. Special tabulation on aging.
　　　　　decennial. IV.25.
AGRICULTURE
　　　Agricultural statistics. annual. V.37.
　　　Residents of farms and rural areas. annual. V.38.
AGUADILLA, PR, MSA
　　　Census tracts. Report no. 59. decennial. I.8.
AKRON, OH, PMSA
　　　Census tracts. Report no. 117A. decennial. I.8.
ALBANY, GA, MSA
　　　Census tracts. Report no. 60. decennial. I.8.
ALBANY-SCHENECTADY-TROY, NY, MSA
　　　Census tracts. Report no. 61. decennial. I.8.

ALBUQUERQUE, NM, MSA
> Census tracts. Report no. 62. decennial. I.8.

ALEUTS
> Census of population. Social and economic characteristics. American
> Indian and Alaska native areas. decennial. IV.15.

ALEXANDRIA, LA, MSA
> Census tracts. Report no. 63. decennial. I.8.

ALGERIA
> Foreign economic trends. annual. II.9.

ALLENTOWN-BETHLEHEM-EASTON, PA-NJ, MSA
> Census tracts. Report no. 64. decennial. I.8.

ALTOONA, PA, MSA
> Census tracts. Report no. 65. decennial. I.8.

AMARILLO, TX, MSA
> Census tracts. Report no. 66. decennial. I.8.

AMERICAN INDIANS *see* INDIANS OF NORTH AMERICA

ANAHEIM-SANTA ANA, CA, PMSA
> Census tracts. Report no. 215A. decennial. I.8.

ANCESTRY GROUPS
> Census of population. Ancestry of the population in the United States.
> decennial. IV.17.

ANCHORAGE, AK, MSA
> Census tracts. Report no. 67. decennial. I.8.

ANDERSON, IN, MSA
> Census tracts. Report no. 68. decennial. I.8.

ANDERSON, SC, MSA
> Census tracts. Report no. 69. decennial. I.8.

ANN ARBOR, MI, PMSA
> Census tracts. Report no. 134A. decennial. I.8.

ANNISTON, AL, MSA
> Census tracts. Report no. 70. decennial. I.8.

APPLETON-OSHKOSH-NEENAH, WI, MSA
> Census tracts. Report no. 71. decennial. I.8.

ARECIBO, PR, MSA
> Census tracts. Report no. 72. decennial. I.8.

ARGENTINA
> Foreign economic trends. annual. II.9.

ARLINGTON, TX *see* FORT WORTH-ARLINGTON, TX, PMSA

ARMED FORCES *see* DEFENSE

ARUBA
> Foreign economic trends. annual. II.9.

ASHEVILLE, NC, MSA
> Census tracts. Report no. 73. decennial. I.8.

ASHLAND, KY *see* HUNTINGTON-ASHLAND, WV-KY-OH, MSA

ASIA, EAST
> Foreign labor trends. annual. I.24.

ASIAN AND PACIFIC ISLANDER AMERICANS
> Asian and Pacific Islander population in the United States. irreg. IV.11.
> Census of population. Asians and Pacific Islanders in the United
> > States. decennial. IV.8.
> Survey of minority-owned business enterprises. Asian Americans,
> > American Indians, and other minorities. quinquennial. V.28.
> We the American...Asians. decennial. IV.9.
> We the American...Pacific Islanders. decennial. IV.10.

ATHENS, GA, MSA
> Census tracts. Report no. 74. decennial. I.8.

ATLANTA, GA, MSA
> Census tracts. Report no. 75. decennial. I.8.

ATLANTIC CITY, NJ, MSA
> Census tracts. Report no. 76. decennial. I.8.

ATTLEBORO, MA *see* PAWTUCKET-WOONSOCKET-ATTLEBORO, RI-MA,
PMSA

AUBURN, ME *see* LEWISTON-AUBURN, ME, MSA

AUGUSTA, GA-SC, MSA
> Census tracts. Report no. 77. decennial. I.8.

AURORA-ELGIN, IL, PMSA
> Census tracts. Report no. 113A. decennial. I.8.

AUSTIN, TX, MSA
> Census tracts. Report no. 78. decennial. I.8.

AUSTRALIA
> Foreign economic trends. annual. II.9.
> Foreign labor trends. annual. I.24.

AUSTRIA
> Foreign economic trends. annual. II.9.
> Foreign labor trends. annual. I.24.

AUTOMOBILE INDUSTRY
> Annual report of the President to the Congress on the operation of the
> > Automotive products trade act of 1965. annual. V.94.
> U.S. automobile industry montly report on selected economic
> > indicators. monthly. V.95.

BAHAMAS
> Foreign economic trends. annual. II.9.

BAHRAIN
>Foreign economic trends. annual. II.9.

BAKERSFIELD, CA, MSA
>Census tracts. Report no. 79. decennial. I.8.

BALTIMORE, MD, MSA
>Census tracts. Report no. 80. decennial. I.8.

BANGLADESH
>Foreign economic trends. annual. II.9.
>Foreign labor trends. annual. I.24.

BANGOR, ME, MSA
>Census tracts. Report no. 81. decennial. I.8.

BARBADOS
>Foreign economic trends. annual. II.9.

BATON ROUGE, LA, MSA
>Census tracts. Report no. 82. decennial. I.8.

BATTLE CREEK, MI, MSA
>Census tracts. Report no. 83. decennial. I.8.

BAY CITY, MI *see* SAGINAW-BAY CITY-MIDLAND, MI, MSA

BEAUMONT-PORT ARTHUR, TX, MSA
>Census tracts. Report no. 84. decennial. I.8.

BEAVER COUNTY, PA, PMSA
>Census tracts. Report no. 262A. decennial. I.8.

BELGIUM
>Foreign economic trends. semiannual. II.9.
>Foreign labor trends. annual. I.24.

BELIZE
>Foreign economic trends. annual. II.9.

BELLINGHAM, WA, MSA
>Census tracts. Report no. 85. decennial. I.8.

BELOIT, WI *see* JANESVILLE-BELOIT, WI, MSA

BENIN
>Foreign economic trends. annual. II.9.

BENTON HARBOR, MI, MSA
>Census tracts. Report no. 86. decennial. I.8.

BERGEN-PASSAIC, NJ, PMSA
>Census tracts. Report no. 245A. decennial. I.8.

BETHLEHEM, PA *see* ALLENTOWN-BETHLEHEM-EASTON, PA-NJ, MSA

BILLINGS, MT, MSA
>Census tracts. Report no. 87. decennial. I.8.

BILOXI-GULFPORT, MS, MSA
>Census tracts. Report no. 88. decennial. I.8.

BINGHAMTON, NY, MSA
Census tracts. Report no. 89. decennial. I.8.
BIRMINGHAM, AL, MSA
Census tracts. Report no. 90. decennial. I.8.
BISMARK, ND, MSA
Census tracts. Report no. 91. decennial. I.8.
BLACK AMERICANS *see* AFRICAN-AMERICANS
BLOOMINGTON, IN, MSA
Census tracts. Report no. 92. decennial. I.8.
BLOOMINGTON-NORMAL, IL, MSA
Census tracts. Report no. 93. decennial. I.8.
BLUE-COLLAR WORKERS
Occupations of federal white-collar and blue-collar workers. biennial.
V.5.
BOCA RATON, FL *see* WEST PALM BEACH-BOCA RATON-DELANY
BEACH, FL, MSA
BOISE CITY, ID, MSA
Census tracts. Report no. 94. decennial. I.8.
BOLIVIA
Foreign economic trends. annual. II.9.
Foreign labor trends. annual. I.24.
BOSTON, MA, PMSA
Census tracts. Report no. 95A. decennial. I.8.
BOSTON-LAWRENCE-SALEM, MA-NH, CMSA
Census tracts. Report nos. 95A-95F. decennial. I.8.
BOTSWANA
Foreign economic trends. annual. II.9.
BOULDER-LONGMONT, CO, PMSA
Census tracts. Report no. 132A. decennial I.8.
BRADENTON, FL, MSA
Census tracts. Report no. 96. decennial. I.8.
BRAZIL
Foreign economic trends. annual. II.9.
Foreign labor trends. annual. I.24.
BRAZORIA, TX, PMSA
Census tracts. Report no. 176A. decennial. I.8.
BREMERTON, WA, MSA
Census tracts. Report no. 97. decennial. I.8.
BRIDGEPORT-MILFORD, CT, PMSA
Census tracts. Report no. 245B. decennial. I.8.
BRIDGETON, NJ *see* VINELAND-MILLVILLE-BRIDGETON, NJ, PMSA

BRISTOL, CT, PMSA
> Census tracts. Report no. 172A. decennial. I.8.

BRISTOL, VA *see* JOHNSON CITY-KINGSPORT-BRISTOL, TN-VA, MSA

BROCKTON, MA, PMSA
> Census tracts. Report no. 95B. decennial. I.8.

BROWNSVILLE-HARLINGEN, TX, MSA
> Census tracts. Report no. 98. decennial. I.8.

BRYAN-COLLEGE STATION, TX, MSA
> Census tracts. Report no. 99. decennial. I.8.

BUFFALO, NY, PMSA
> Census tracts. Report no. 100A. decennial. I.8.

BUFFALO-NIAGARA FALLS, NY, CMSA
> Census tracts. Report nos. 100A-100B. decennial. I.8.

BULGARIA
> Foreign economic trends. annual. II.9.

BURKINA FASO
> Foreign economic trends. annual. II.9.

BURLINGTON, NC, MSA
> Census tracts. Report no. 101. decennial. I.8.

BURLINGTON, VT, MSA
> Census tracts. Report no. 102. decennial. I.8.

BURMA
> Foreign economic trends. annual. II.9.

BURUNDI
> Foreign economic trends. annual. II.9.

CAGUAS, PR, PMSA
> Census tracts. Report no. 295A. decennial. I.8.

CAMEROON
> Foreign economic trends. annual. II.9.

CANADA
> Foreign economic trends. semiannual. II.9.
> Foreign labor trends. annual. I.24.

CANTON, OH, MSA
> Census tracts. Report no. 103. decennial. I.8.

CAPE CORAL, FL *see* FORT MYERS-CAPE CORAL, FL, MSA

CAPE VERDE
> Foreign economic trends. annual. II.9.

CAREERS *see* OCCUPATIONS; *and specific occupations or careers, e.g.,*
> ENGINEERS, PHYSICIANS, SCIENTISTS

CARIBBEAN, EASTERN
> Foreign labor trends. annual. I.24.

CARLISLE, PA *see* HARRISBURG-LEBANON-CARLISLE, PA, MSA
CASPER, WY, MSA
      Census tracts. Report no. 104. decennial. I.8.
CEDAR FALLS, IA *see* WATERLOO-CEDAR FALLS, IA, MSA
CEDAR RAPIDS, IA, MSA
      Census tracts. Report no. 105. decennial. I.8.
CENTRAL AFRICAN REPUBLIC
      Foreign economic trends. annual. II.9.
CHAD
      Foreign economic trends. annual. II.9.
CHAMPAIGN-URBANA-RANTOUL, IL, MSA
      Census tracts. Report no. 106. decennial. I.8.
CHARLESTON, SC, MSA
      Census tracts. Report no. 107. decennial. I.8.
CHARLESTON, WV, MSA
      Census tracts. Report no. 108. decennial. I.8.
CHARLOTTE-GASTONIA-ROCK HILL, NC-SC, MSA
      Census tracts. Report no. 109. decennial. I.8.
CHARLOTTESVILLE, VA, MSA
      Census tracts. Report no. 110. decennial. I.8.
CHATTANOOGA, TN-GA, MSA
      Census tracts. Report no. 111. decennial. I.8.
CHEYENNE, WY, MSA
      Census tracts. Report no. 112. decennial. I.8.
CHICAGO, IL, PMSA
      Census tracts. Report no. 113B. decennial. I.8.
CHICAGO-GARY-LAKE COUNTY, IL-IN-WI, CMSA
      Census tracts. Report nos. 113A-113F. decennial. I.8.
CHICO, CA, MSA
      Census tracts. Report no. 114. decennial. I.8.
CHILD LABOR
      Foreign labor trends. annual. I.24.
CHILE
      Foreign economic trends. semiannual. II.9.
      Foreign labor trends. annual. I.24.
CHINA (PEOPLE'S REPUBLIC OF)
      Foreign economic trends. annual. II.9.
      Foreign labor trends. annual. I.24.
CINCINNATI, OH-KY-IN, PMSA
      Census tracts. Report no. 115A. decennial. I.8.

CINCINNATI-HAMILTON, OH-KY-IN, CMSA
   Census tracts. Report nos. 115A-115B. decennial. I.8.
CITIES *see* UNITED STATES—NATIONAL, STATES, COUNTIES/
   METROPOLITAN AREAS, CITIES; *and other subdivisions under*
   UNITED STATES; *also names of individual cities or metropolitan*
   areas, e.g., ABILENE, TX, MSA; BURLINGTON, VT, MSA
CLARKSVILLE-HOPKINSVILLE, TN-KY, MSA
   Census tracts. Report no. 116. decennial. I.8.
CLEARWATER, FL *see* TAMPA-ST. PETERSBURG-CLEARWATER, FL, MSA
CLEVELAND, OH, PMSA
   Census tracts. Report no. 117B. decennial. I.8.
CLEVELAND-AKRON-LORAIN, OH, CMSA
   Census tracts. Report nos. 117A-117C. decennial. I.8.
COAL MINING
   Coal production. annual. V.59.
COLLEGE STATION, TX *see* BRYAN-COLLEGE STATION, TX, MSA
COLOMBIA
   Foreign economic trends. annual. II.9.
   Foreign labor trends. annual. I.24.
COLORADO SPRINGS, CO, MSA
   Census tracts. Report no. 118. decennial. I.8.
COLUMBIA, MO, MSA
   Census tracts. Report no. 119. decennial. I.8.
COLUMBIA, SC, MSA
   Census tracts. Report no. 120. decennial. I.8.
COLUMBUS, GA-AL, MSA
   Census tracts. Report no. 121. decennial. I.8.
COLUMBUS, OH, MSA
   Census tracts. Report no. 122. decennial. I.8.
CONGO
   Foreign economic trends. annual. II.9.
CONGRESSIONAL DISTRICTS *see* UNITED STATES—CONGRESSIONAL
   DISTRICTS
CONSTRUCTION INDUSTRY
   Census of construction industries. Geographic area series. quinquennial.
      V.40.
   Census of construction industries. Industry series. quinquennial. V.41.
   Construction review. quarterly. V.39.
   Occupational employment in mining, construction, finance, and
      services. triennial. V.26.

CORPUS CHRISTI, TX, MSA
> Census tracts. Report no. 123. decennial. I.8.

CORRECTIONS *see* CRIMINAL JUSTICE

COSTA RICA
> Foreign economic trends. annual. II.9.
> Foreign labor trends. annual. I.24.

COUNTIES *see* UNITED STATES—NATIONAL, STATES, COUNTIES/
METROPOLITAN AREAS, CITIES; *and other subdivisions under*
UNITED STATES; *also names of individual counties or metropolitan*
areas, e.g., ABILENE, TX, MSA; BURLINGTON, VT, MSA

CRIMINAL JUSTICE
> Children in custody. biennial. V.43.
> Sourcebook of criminal justice statistics. annual. V.42.

CUMBERLAND, MD-WV, MSA
> Census tracts. Report no. 124. decennial. I.8.

CYPRUS
> Foreign economic trends. annual. II.9.

CZECHOSLOVAKIA
> Foreign economic trends. annual. II.9.

DALLAS, TX, PMSA
> Census tracts. Report no. 125A. decennial. I.8.

DALLAS-FORT WORTH, TX, CMSA
> Census tracts. Report nos. 125A-125B. decennial. I.8.

DANBURY, CT, PMSA
> Census tracts. Report no. 245C. decennial. I.8.

DANVILLE, VA, MSA
> Census tracts. Report no. 126. decennial. I.8.

DAVENPORT-ROCK ISLAND-MOLINE, IA-IL, MSA
> Census tracts. Report no. 127. decennial. I.8.

DAYTON-SPRINGFIELD, OH, MSA
> Census tracts. Report no. 128. decennial. I.8.

DAYTONA BEACH, FL, MSA
> Census tracts. Report no. 129. decennial. I.8.

DECATUR, AL, MSA
> Census tracts. Report no. 130. decennial. I.8.

DECATUR, IL, MSA
> Census tracts. Report no. 131. decennial. I.8.

DEFENSE
> Defense almanac. annual. V.7.
> Department of Defense selected manpower statistics. annual. V.8.

Military manpower statistics. quarterly. V.6.
Projected defense purchases: detail by industry and state. biennial. V.9.
DELRAY BEACH *see* WEST PALM BEACH-BOCA RATON-DELRAY BEACH,
       FL, MSA
DENISON, TX *see* SHERMAN-DENISON, TX, MSA
DENMARK
       Foreign labor trends. annual. I.24.
DENTISTS
       Factbook: Health personnel, U.S. biennial. V.53.
DENVER, CO, PMSA
       Census tracts. Report no. 132B. decennial. I.8.
DENVER-BOULDER, CO, CMSA
       Census tracts. Report nos. 132A-132B. decennial. I.8.
DES MOINES, IA, MSA
       Census tracts. Report no. 133. decennial. I.8.
DETROIT, MI, PMSA
       Census tracts. Report no. 134B. decennial. I.8.
DETROIT-ANN ARBOR, MI, CMSA
       Census tracts. Report nos. 134A-134B. decennial. I.8.
DISABLED
       Affirmative employment statistics. biennial. V.3.
       Annual report on the employment of minorities, women, and people with
              disabilities in the federal government. annual. V.2.
       Chartbook on work disability in the United States. irreg. IV.27.
       Labor force status and other characteristics of persons with a work
              disability: 1981-1988. irreg. IV.28.
DOMINICAN REPUBLIC
       Foreign labor trends. annual. I.24.
DOTHAN, AL, MSA
       Census tracts. Report no. 135. decennial. I.8.
DOVER, NH *see* PORTSMOUTH-DOVER-ROCHESTER, NH-ME, MSA
DUBUQUE, IA, MSA
       Census tracts. Report no. 136. decennial. I.8.
DULUTH, MN-WI, MSA
       Census tracts. Report no. 137. decennial. I.8.
DUNKIRK, NY *see* JAMESTOWN-DUNKIRK, NY, MSA
DURHAM, NC *see* RALEIGH-DURHAM, NC, MSA
EASTON, PA *see* ALLENTOWN-BETHLEHEM-EASTON, PA-NJ, MSA
EAU CLAIRE, WI, MSA
       Census tracts. Report no. 138. decennial. I.8.

ECUADOR

    Foreign economic trends. semiannual. II.9.

    Foreign labor trends. annual. I.24.

EDINBURG, TX *see* McALLEN-EDINBURG-MISSION, TX, MSA

EDUCATION

    Condition of education. annual. V.44.

    Digest of education statistics. annual. V.45.

    Projections of education statistics. annual. V.46.

    Salaries of full-time instructional faculty on 9- and 10-month contracts
        in institutions of higher education. annual. V.47.

    State higher education profiles. annual. V.48.

    State profiles of public elementary and secondary education. biennial.
        V.49.

EGYPT

    Foreign economic trends. annual. II.9.

    Foreign labor trends. annual. I.24.

EL PASO, TX, MSA

    Census tracts. Report no. 139. decennial. I.8.

EL SALVADOR

    Foreign economic trends. annual. II.9.

    Foreign labor trends. annual. I.24.

ELGIN, IL *see* AURORA-ELGIN, IL, PMSA

ELKHART-GOSHEN, IN, MSA

    Census tracts. Report no. 140. decennial. I.8.

ELMIRA, NY, MSA

    Census tracts. Report no. 141. decennial. I.8.

ELYRIA, OH *see* LORAIN-ELYRIA, OH, PMSA

EMPLOYMENT PROJECTIONS

    The American workforce: 1992-2005. III.3.

    BEA regional projections to 2040. quinquennial. III.6.

    Career guide to industries. annual. III.2, V.19.

    Occupational outlook handbook. biennial. III.4, V.24.

    Occupational outlook quarterly. quarterly. III.1, V.17.

    Occupational projections and training data, a statistical and research
        supplement to Occupational outlook handbook. biennial. III.5,
        V.25.

ENGINEERING

    Science and engineering indicators. annual. V.70.

    Women and minorities in science and engineering. biennial. V.72.

ENGINEERS

    Characteristics of doctoral scientists and engineers in the U.S.
        biennial. V.69.

FAYETTEVILLE-SPRINGDALE, AR, MSA
>   Census tracts. Report no. 148. decennial. I.8.

FIJI
>   Foreign economic trends. annual. II.9.

FINANCE
>   Occupational employment in mining, construction, finance, and
>   services. triennial. V.26.

FINLAND
>   Foreign economic trends. annual. II.9.
>   Foreign labor trends. annual. I.24.

FISHERIES
>   Fisheries of the U.S. annual. V.50.

FITCHBURG-LEOMINSTER, MA, MSA
>   Census tracts. Report no. 149. decennial. I.8.

FLINT, MI, MSA
>   Census tracts. Report no. 150. decennial. I.8.

FLORENCE, AL, MSA
>   Census tracts. Report no. 151. decennial. I.8.

FLORENCE, SC, MSA
>   Census tracts. Report no. 152. decennial. I.8.

FORECASTING *see* EMPLOYMENT PROJECTIONS

FOREIGN BORN
>   Census of population. Ancestry of the population in the United States.
>   decennial. V.17.
>   Census of population. The foreign-born population in the United
>   States. decennial. IV.18.
>   We the American...foreign born. decennial. IV.19.

FOREIGN COUNTRIES
>   Country reports on economic policy and trade practices. annual. II.8.
>   Economic report of the President. annual. I.23.
>   Foreign economic trends and their implications for the United States.
>   annual or semiannual. II.9.
>   Foreign labor trends. annual. I.24.
>   Handbook of economic statistics. annual. II.10.
>   Handbook of labor statistics. irreg. I.19.
>   Monthly labor review. monthly. I.3.
>   Statistical abstract of the United States. annual. I.5.
>   The world factbook. annual. II.11.
>   *see also specific countries, e.g.,* AUSTRALIA, DENMARK

FOREIGN INVESTMENT—UNITED STATES
>   Foreign direct investment in the United States. Operations of U.S.
>   affiliates of foreign companies. annual. V.21.

News. Employment and wages in foreign-owned businesses in the United States. quarterly. V.16.

FOREIGN TRADE

Trade and employment. quarterly. V.18.

U.S. manufactured exports and export-related employment. annual. V.87.

see also EXPORTS

FORT COLLINS-LOVELAND, CO, MSA

Census tracts. Report no. 153. decennial. I.8.

FORT LAUDERDALE-HOLLYWOOD-POMPANO BEACH, FL, PMSA

Census tracts. Report no. 229A. decennial. I.8.

FORT MYERS-CAPE CORAL, FL, MSA

Census tracts. Report no. 154. decennial. I.8.

FORT PIERCE, FL, MSA

Census tracts. Report no. 155. decennial. I.8.

FORT SMITH, AR-OK, MSA

Census tracts. Report no. 156. decennial. I.8.

FORT WALTON BEACH, FL, MSA

Census tracts. Report no. 157. decennial. I.8.

FORT WAYNE, IN, MSA

Census tracts. Report no. 158. decennial. I.8.

FORT WORTH-ARLINGTON, TX, PMSA

Census tracts. Report no. 125B. decennial. I.8.

FRANCE

Foreign economic trends. semiannual. II.9.

Foreign labor trends. annual. I.24.

FRESNO, CA, MSA

Census tracts. Report no. 159. decennial. I.8.

GABON

Foreign economic trends. annual. II.9.

GADSDEN, AL, MSA

Census tracts. Report no. 160. decennial I.8.

GAINESVILLE, FL, MSA

Census tracts. Report no. 161. decennial. I.8.

GALVESTON-TEXAS CITY, TX, PMSA

Census tracts. Report no. 176B. decennial. I.8.

GARY-HAMMOND, IN, PMSA

Census tracts. Report no. 113C. decennial. I.8.

GASTONIA, NC *see* CHARLOTTE-GASTONIA-ROCK HILL, NC-SC, MSA

GERMANY
> Foreign economic trends. annual. II.9.
> Foreign labor trends. annual. I.24.

GHANA
> Foreign economic trends. annual. II.9.
> Foreign labor trends. annual. I.24.

GLENS FALLS, NY, MSA
> Census tracts. Report no. 162. decennial. I.8.

GLOUCESTER, MA *see* SALEM-GLOUCESTER, MA, PMSA

GOSHEN, IN, MSA *see* ELKHART-GOSHEN, IN, MSA

GOVERNMENT—FEDERAL GOVERNMENT
> Affirmative employment statistics. biennial. V.3.
> Annual report on the employment of minorities, women, and people with disabilities in the federal government. annual. V.2.
> Biennial report of employment by geographic area. biennial. V.4.
> Employment and trends. bimonthly. V.1.
> Manufacturers shipments to the federal government. quinquennial. V.92.
> Occupations of federal white-collar and blue-collar workers. biennial. V.5.
> *see also* DEFENSE; POSTAL SERVICE

GOVERNMENT—STATE, COUNTY, LOCAL
> Census of governments. Public employment. quinquennial. V.15.
> City employment. annual. V.11.
> County government employment. annual. V.12.
> Job patterns for minorities and women in state and local government. annual. V.13.
> Public employment. Government employment. annual. V.14.

GRAND FORKS, ND, MSA
> Census tracts. Report no. 163. decennial. I.8.

GRAND RAPIDS, MI, MSA
> Census tracts. Report no. 164. decennial. I.8.

GREAT FALLS, MT, MSA
> Census tracts. Report no. 165. decennial. I.8.

GREECE
> Foreign economic trends. annual. II.9.
> Foreign labor trends. annual. I.24.

GREELEY, CO, MSA
> Census tracts. Report no. 166. decennial. I.8.

GREEN BAY, WI, MSA
> Census tracts. Report no. 167. decennial. I.8.

GREENSBORO-WINSTON-SALEM-HIGH POINT, NC, MSA
 Census tracts. Report no. 168. decennial. I.8.
GREENVILLE-SPARTANBURG, SC, MSA
 Census tracts. Report no. 169. decennial. I.8.
GRENADA
 Foreign economic trends. annual. II.9.
GUATEMALA
 Foreign economic trends. annual. II.9.
GUINEA
 Foreign economic trends. annual. II.9.
GULFPORT, MS *see* BILOXI-GULFPORT, MS, MSA
GUYANA
 Foreign economic trends. annual. II.9.
 Foreign labor trends. annual. I.24.
HAGERSTOWN, MD, MSA
 Census tracts. Report no. 170. decennial. I.8.
HAITI
 Foreign economic trends. annual. II.9.
 Foreign labor trends. annual. I.24.
HAMILTON-MIDDLETOWN, OH, PMSA
 Census tracts. Report no. 115B. decennial. I.8.
HAMMOND, IN *see* GARY-HAMMOND, IN, PMSA
HANDICAPPED *see* DISABLED
HARLINGEN, TX *see* BROWNSVILLE-HARLINGEN, TX, MSA
HARRISBURG-LEBANON-CARLISLE, PA, MSA
 Census tracts. Report no. 171. decennial. I.8.
HARTFORD, CT, PMSA
 Census tracts. Report no. 172B. decennial. I.8.
HARTFORD-NEW BRITAIN-MIDDLETOWN, CT, CMSA
 Census tracts. Report nos. 172A-172D. decennial. I.8.
HAVERHILL, MA *see* LAWRENCE-HAVERHILL, MA-NH, PMSA
HEALTH CARE
 Health care financing review. quarterly. V.51.
 Health U.S., and prevention profile. annual. V.52.
 Factbook: Health personnel, U.S. biennial. V.53.
 see also MEDICAL PERSONNEL
HEALTH OCCUPATIONS *see* HEALTH CARE; MEDICAL PERSONNEL
HIALEAH, FL *see* MIAMI-HIALEAH, FL, PMSA
HICKORY-MORGANTON, NC, MSA
 Census tracts. Report no. 173. decennial. I.8.

HIGH POINT, NC *see* GREENSBORO-WINSTON-SALEM-HIGHPOINT,
    NC, MSA

HISPANIC AMERICANS
    Census of population. Persons of Hispanic origin in the United States.
        decennial. IV.14.
    The Hispanic population of the United States. annual. IV.13.
    Noticias de la semana. weekly. IV.12.
    Survey of minority-owned business enterprises. Hispanic. quinquennial.
        V.30.
    We the American...Hispanics. IV.14A.

HOLLYWOOD, FL *see* FORT LAUDERDALE-HOLLYWOOD-POMPANO
    BEACH, FL, PMSA

HONDURAS
    Foreign economic trends. annual. II.9.
    Foreign labor trends. annual. I.24.

HONG KONG
    Foreign economic trends. annual. II.9.
    Foreign labor trends. annual. I.24.

HONOLULU, HI, MSA
    Census tracts. Report no. 174. decennial. I.8.

HOPKINSVILLE, KY *see* CLARKSVILLE-HOPKINSVILLE, TN-KY, MSA

HOUMA-THIBODAUX, LA, MSA
    Census tracts. Report no. 175. decennial. I.8.

HOUSTON, TX, PMSA
    Census tracts. Report no. 176C. decennial. I.8.

HOUSTON-GALVESTON-BRAZORIA, TX, CMSA
    Census tracts. Report nos. 176A-176C. decennial. I.8.

HUNGARY
    Foreign economic trends. annual. II.9.

HUNTERDON, NJ *see* MIDDLESEX-SOMERSET-HUNTERDON, NJ, PMSA

HUNTINGTON-ASHLAND, WV-KY-OH, MSA
    Census tracts. Report no. 177. decennial. I.8.

HUNTSVILLE, AL, MSA
    Census tracts. Report no. 178. decennial. I.8.

ICELAND
    Foreign economic trends. annual. II.9.
    Foreign labor trends. annual. I.24.

IMMIGRANTS
    Census of population. Ancestry of the population in the United States.
        decennial. IV.17.
    Census of population. The foreign-born population in the United
        States. decennial. IV.18.

President's comprehensive triennial report on immigration. triennial.
IV.29.

We the American...foreign born. decennial. IV.19.

INDIA

Foreign economic trends. annual. II.9.

Foreign labor trends. annual. I.24.

INDIANAPOLIS, IN, MSA

Census tracts. Report no. 179. decennial. I.8.

INDIANS OF NORTH AMERICA

Census of population. Characteristics of American Indians by tribe and
language. decennial. IV.14B.

Census of population. Social and economic characteristics. American
Indian and Alaska native areas. decennial. IV.15.

Survey of minority-owned business enterprises. Asian Americans,
American Indians, and other minorities. quinquennial. V.28.

We the...first Americans. decennial. IV.16.

INDONESIA

Foreign economic trends. semiannual. II.9.

Foreign labor trends. annual. I.24.

INDUSTRIES

Career guide to industries. annual. III.2, V.19.

Company summary. Enterprise statistics. quinquennial. V.33.

County business patterns. annual. V.20.

Foreign direct investment in the United States. Operations of U.S.
affiliates of foreign companies. annual. V.21.

Large companies. Enterprise statistics. quinquennial. V.34.

News. Employment and wages in foreign-owned businesses in the
United States. quarterly. V.16.

The state of small business. annual. V.22.

Survey of minority business enterprises. Asian Americans, American
Indians, and other minorities. quinquennial. V.28.

Survey of minority-owned business enterprises. Black. quinquennial.
V.29.

Survey of minority-owned business enterprises. Hispanic. quinquennial.
V.30.

Survey of minority-owned business enterprises. Summary. quinquennial.
V.31.

Trade and employment. quarterly. V.18.

U.S. industrial outlook. annual. V.23.

Women-owned businesses. quinquennial. V.32.

see also specific industries, e.g., CONSTRUCTION INDUSTRY;
DEPARTMENT STORES; MANUFACTURING

INTERNATIONAL LABOR ACTIVITIES
        Foreign labor trends. annual. I.24.
IOWA CITY, IA, MSA
        Census tracts. Report no. 180. decennial. I.8.
IRELAND
        Foreign economic trends. annual. II.9.
        Foreign labor trends. annual. I.24.
ISRAEL
        Foreign economic trends. annual. II.9.
ITALY
        Foreign economic trends. annual. II.9.
        Foreign labor trends. annual. I.24.
IVORY COAST
        Foreign economic trends. annual. II.9.
JACKSON, MI, MSA
        Census tracts. Report no. 181. decennial. I.8.
JACKSON, MS, MSA
        Census tracts. Report no. 182. decennial. I.8.
JACKSON, TN, MSA
        Census tracts. Report no. 183. decennial. I.8.
JACKSONVILLE, FL, MSA
        Census tracts. Report no. 184. decennial. I.8.
JACKSONVILLE, NC, MSA
        Census tracts. Report no. 185. decennial. I.8.
JAMAICA
        Foreign economic trends. annual. II.9.
        Foreign labor trends. annual. I.24.
JAMESTOWN-DUNKIRK, NY, MSA
        Census tracts. Report no. 186. decennial. I.8.
JANESVILLE-BELOIT, WI, MSA
        Census tracts. Report no. 187. decennial. I.8.
JAPAN
        Foreign economic trends. semiannual. II.9.
        Foreign labor trends. annual. I.24.
JERSEY CITY, NJ, PMSA
        Census tracts. Report no. 245D. decennial. I.8.
JOHNSON CITY-KINGSPORT-BRISTOL, TN-VA, MSA
        Census tracts. Report no. 188. decennial. I.8.
JOHNSTOWN, PA, MSA
        Census tracts. Report no. 189. decennial. I.8.

JOLIET, IL, PMSA
>Census tracts. Report no. 113D. decennial. I.8.

JOPLIN, MO, MSA
>Census tracts. Report no. 190. decennial. I.8.

JORDAN
>Foreign economic trends. annual. II.9.
>Foreign labor trends. annual. I.24.

JUSTICE
>Justice expenditure and employment in the U.S. annual. V.54.
>*see also* CRIMINAL JUSTICE; LAW ENFORCEMENT

KALAMAZOO, MI, MSA
>Census tracts. Report no. 191. decennial. I.8.

KANKAKEE, IL, MSA
>Census tracts. Report no. 192. decennial. I.8.

KANSAS CITY, MO-KS, MSA
>Census tracts. Report no. 193. decennial. I.8.

KENNEWICK, WA *see* RICHLAND-KENNEWICK-PASCO, WA, MSA

KENOSHA, WI, PMSA
>Census tracts. Report no. 113E. decennial. I.8.

KENYA
>Foreign economic trends. annual. II.9.
>Foreign labor trends. annual. I.24.

KILLEEN-TEMPLE, TX, MSA
>Census tracts. Report no. 194. decennial. I.8.

KINGSPORT, TN *see* JOHNSON CITY-KINGSPORT-BRISTOL, TN-VA, MSA

KNOXVILLE, TN, MSA
>Census tracts. Report no. 195. decennial. I.8.

KOKOMO, IN, MSA
>Census tracts. Report no. 196. decennial. I.8.

KOREA
>Foreign economic trends. annual. II.9.
>Foreign labor trends. annual. I.24.

KUWAIT
>Foreign economic trends. annual. II.9.
>Foreign labor trends. annual. I.24.

LA CROSSE, WI, MSA
>Census tracts. Report no. 197. decennial. I.8.

LAFAYETTE, LA, MSA
>Census tracts. Report no. 198. decennial. I.8.

LAFAYETTE-WEST LAFAYETTE, IN, MSA
Census tracts. Report no. 199. decennial. I.8.
LAKE CHARLES, LA, MSA
Census tracts. Report no. 200. decennial. I.8.
LAKE COUNTY, IL, PMSA
Census tracts. Report no. 113F. decennial. I.8.
LAKELAND-WINTER HAVEN, FL, MSA
Census tracts. Report no. 201. decennial. I.8.
LANCASTER, PA, MSA
Census tracts. Report no. 202. decennial. I.8.
LANSING-EAST LANSING, MI, MSA
Census tracts. Report no. 203. decennial. I.8.
LAOS
Foreign economic trends. annual. II.9.
LAREDO, TX, MSA
Census tracts. Report no. 204. decennial. I.8.
LAS CRUCES, NM, MSA
Census tracts. Report no. 205. decennial. I.8.
LAS VEGAS, NV, MSA
Census tracts. Report no. 206. decennial. I.8.
LATIN AMERICA
Foreign labor trends. annual. I.24.
LATIN AMERICANS *see* HISPANIC AMERICANS
LAW ENFORCEMENT
Profiles of state and local law enforcement agencies. irreg. V.57.
Sheriffs' departments; a LEMAS report. triennial. V.56,
Uniform crime reports: crime in the U.S. annual. V.55.
LAWRENCE, KS, MSA
Census tracts. Report no. 207. decennial. I.8.
LAWRENCE-HAVERHILL, MA-NH, PMSA
Census tracts. Report no. 95C. decennial. I.8.
LAWTON, OK, MSA
Census tracts. Report no. 208. decennial. I.8.
LEBANON, PA *see* HARRISBURG-LEBANON-CARLISLE, PA, MSA
LEOMINSTER, MA *see* FITCHBURG-LEOMINSTER, MA, MSA
LESOTHO
Foreign economic trends. annual. II.9.
LEWISTON-AUBURN, ME, MSA
Census tracts. Report no. 209. decennial. I.8.
LEXINGTON-FAYETTE, KY, MSA
Census tracts. Report no. 210. decennial. I.8.

LIBERIA
    Foreign economic trends. annual. II.9.
    Foreign labor trends. annual. I.24.
LIBRARIANS
    Digest of education statistics. annual. V.45.
LIMA, OH, MSA
    Census tracts. Report no. 211. decennial. I.8.
LINCOLN, NE, MSA
    Census tracts. Report no. 212. decennial. I.8.
LITTLE ROCK-NORTH LITTLE ROCK, AR, MSA
    Census tracts. Report no. 213. decennial. I.8.
LOMPOC, CA *see* SANTA BARBARA-SANTA MARIA-LOMPOC, CA, MSA
LONG BEACH, CA *see* LOS ANGELES-LONG BEACH, CA, PMSA
LONGMONT, CO, PMSA *see* BOULDER-LONGMONT, CO, PMSA
LONGVIEW-MARSHALL, TX , MSA
    Census tracts. Report no. 214. decennial. I.8.
LORAIN-ELYRIA, OH, PMSA
    Census tracts. Report no. 117C. decennial. I.8.
LOS ANGELES-ANAHEIM-RIVERSIDE, CA, CMSA
    Census tracts. Report nos. 215A-215D. decennial. I.8.
LOS ANGELES-LONG BEACH, CA, PMSA
    Census tracts. Report no. 215B. decennial. I.8.
LOUISVILLE, KY-IN, MSA
    Census tracts. Report no. 216. decennial. I.8.
LOVELAND, CO *see* FORT COLLINS-LOVELAND, CO, MSA
LOWELL, MA-NH, PMSA
    Census tracts. Report no. 95D. decennial. I.8.
LUBBOCK, TX, MSA
    Census tracts. Report no. 217. decennial. I.8.
LUMBER INDUSTRY
    Bulletin of hardwood market statistics. quarterly. V.58.
LUXEMBOURG
    Foreign economic trends. annual. II.9.
LYNCHBURG, VA, MSA
    Census tracts. Report no. 218. decennial. I.8.
MACON-WARNER ROBINS, GA, MSA
    Census tracts. Report no. 219. decennial. I.8.
MADAGASCAR
    Foreign economic trends. annual. II.9.
MADISON, WI, MSA
    Census tracts. Report no. 220. decennial. I.8.

MALAWI
>Foreign economic trends. annual. II.9.

MALAYSIA
>Foreign economic trends. annual. II.9.
>Foreign labor trends. annual. I.24.

MALI
>Foreign economic trends. annual. II.9.

MANCHESTER, NH, MSA
>Census tracts. Report no. 221. decennial. I.8.

MANSFIELD, OH, MSA
>Census tracts. Report no. 222. decennial. I.8.

MANUFACTURING INDUSTRIES
>Annual survey of manufactures. Geographic area statistics. annual.
>>V.84.
>Annual survey of manufactures. Statistics for industry groups and
>>industries. annual. V.85.
>Census of manufactures. Geographic area series. quinquennial. V.90.
>Census of manufactures. Industry series. quinquennial. V.91.
>Census of manufactures. Subject series. General summary: industry
>>product class. quinquennial. V.92.
>Census of manufactures. Subject series. Manufacturers
>>shipments to the federal government. quinquennial. V.92.
>Census of manufactures. Subject series. Type of organization.
>>quinquennial. V.92.
>Employment, hours & earnings, United States, 1909-94. irreg. I.17.
>Exports from manufacturing establishments. Manufacturing: analytical
>>report series. annual. V.86.
>Occupational employment in manufacturing industries. triennial.
>>V.88.
>Scientists, engineers and technicians in manufacturing
>>industries: detailed statistical tables. triennial. V.89.
>Selected characteristics of manufacturing establishments that export.
>>Manufacturing analytical report series. quinquennial. V.93.
>U.S. manufactured exports and export-related employment.
>>annual. V.87.
>*see also specific manufacturing industries, e.g.,* AUTOMOBILE
>>INDUSTRY; STEEL INDUSTRY

MARIETTA, OH *see* PARKERSBURG-MARIETTA, WV-OH, MSA

MARSHALL, TX *see* LONGVIEW-MARSHALL, TX, MSA

MASS MEDIA
>Occupational employment in transportation, communications,
>>utilities, and trade. irreg. V.36.

MAURITANIA
> Foreign economic trends, annual. II.9.

MAURITIUS
> Foreign economic trends. annual. II.9.

MAYAGUEZ, PR, MSA
> Census tracts. Report no. 223. decennial. I.8.

McALLEN-EDINBURG-MISSION, TX, MSA
> Census tracts. Report no. 224. decennial. I.8.

MEDFORD, OR, MSA
> Census tracts. Report no. 225. decennial. I.8.

MEDICAL CARE *see* HEALTH CARE

MEDICAL PERSONNEL
> Factbook: Health personnel, U.S. biennial. V.53.
> *see also* HEALTH CARE; PHYSICIANS

MELBOURNE-TITUSVILLE-PALM BAY, FL, MSA
> Census tracts. Report no. 226. decennial. I.8.

MEMPHIS, TN-AR-MS, MSA
> Census tracts. Report no. 227. decennial. I.8.

MERCED, CA, MSA
> Census tracts. Report no. 228. decennial. I.8.

MERIDEN *see* NEW HAVEN-MERIDEN, CT, MSA

MEXICAN AMERICANS *see* HISPANIC AMERICANS

MEXICO
> Foreign economic trends. annual. II.9.
> Foreign labor trends. annual. I.24.

MIAMI-FORT LAUDERDALE, FL, CMSA
> Census tracts. Report nos. 229A-229B. decennial. I.8.

MIAMI-HIALEAH, FL, PMSA
> Census tracts. Report no. 229B. decennial. I.8.

MIDDLESEX-SOMERSET-HUNTERDON, NJ, PMSA
> Census tracts. Report no. 245E. decennial. I.8.

MIDDLETOWN, CT, PMSA
> Census tracts. Report no. 172C. decennial. I.8.

MIDDLETOWN, OH *see* HAMILTON-MIDDLETOWN, OH, PMSA

MIDLAND, MI *see* SAGINAW-BAY CITY-MIDLAND, MI, MSA

MIDLAND, TX, MSA
> Census tracts. Report no. 230. decennial. I.8.

MILFORD, CT *see* BRIDGEPORT-MILFORD, CT, PMSA

MILITARY PERSONNEL *see* DEFENSE

MILLVILLE, NJ *see* VINELAND-MILLVILLE-BRIDGETON, NJ, PMSA

MILWAUKEE, WI, PMSA
> Census tracts. Report no. 231A. decennial. I.8.

MILWAUKEE-RACINE, WI, CMSA
> Census tracts. Report nos. 231A-231B. decennial. I.8.

MINERAL INDUSTRIES
> Census of mineral industries. Geographic area series. quinquennial.
>> V.62.

> Census of mineral industries. Industry series. quinquennial. V.63.
> Census of mineral industries. Subject series. quinquennial. V.64.
> Mineral commodity summaries. annual. V.60.

> Minerals yearbook. annual. V.61.
> *see also* MINING

MINING
> Occupational employment in mining, construction, finance, and
>> services. triennial. V.26.

> *see also* COAL MINING; MINERAL INDUSTRIES

MINNEAPOLIS-ST. PAUL, MN-WI, MSA
> Census tracts. Report no. 232. decennial. I.8.

MINORITIES
> Affirmative employment statistics. Federal civilian workforce
>> statistics. biennial. V.3.

> Annual report on the employment of minorities, women, and people with
>> disabilities in the federal government. annual. V.2.

> Employment in perspective: minority workers. quarterly. IV.1.
> Equal employment opportunity file. decennial. IV.4.
> Job patterns for minorities and women in private industry. annual.
>> IV.2.

> Job patterns for minorities and women in state and local government.
>> annual. V.13.

> Reports to the Congress required by the Fair labor standards act.
>> annual. IV.3.

> Survey of minority-owned business enterprises. Asian Americans,
>> American Indians, and other minorities. quinquennial. V.28.

> Survey of minority-owned business enterprises. Summary. quinquennial.
>> V.31.

> Women and minorities in science and engineering. biennial. V.72.
> *see also specific minorities, e.g.,* AFRICAN-AMERICANS; ASIAN AND
>> PACIFIC ISLANDER AMERICANS; HISPANIC AMERICANS,
>> etc.

MISHAWAKA, IN, MSA *see* SOUTH BEND-MISHAWAKA, IN, MSA
MISSION, TX *see* McALLEN-EDINBURG-MISSION, TX, MSA
MOBILE, AL, MSA
> Census tracts. Report no. 233. decennial. I.8.

MODESTO, CA, MSA
> Census tracts. Report no. 234. decennial. I.8.

MOLINE, IL *see* DAVENPORT-ROCK ISLAND-MOLINE, IA-IL, MSA

MONMOUTH-OCEAN, NJ, PMSA
> Census tracts. Report no. 245F. decennial. I.8.

MONROE, LA, MSA
> Census tracts. Report no. 235. decennial. I.8.

MONTEREY, CA *see* SALINAS-SEASIDE-MONTEREY, CA, MSA

MONTGOMERY, AL, MSA
> Census tracts. Report no. 236. decennial. I.8.

MOORHEAD, MN *see* FARGO-MOORHEAD, ND-MN, MSA

MORGANTOWN, NC *see* HICKORY-MORGANTOWN, NC, MSA

MOROCCO
> Foreign economic trends. annual. II.9.
> Foreign labor trends. annual. I.24.

MOZAMBIQUE
> Foreign economic trends. annual. II.9.

MUNCIE, IN, MSA
> Census tracts. Report no. 237. decennial. I.8.

MUSKEGON, MI, MSA
> Census tracts. Report no. 238. decennial. I.8.

NAMIBIA
> Foreign economic trends. annual. II.9.

NAPA, CA *see* VALLEJO-FAIRFIELD-NAPA, CA, PMSA

NAPLES, FL, MSA
> Census tracts. Report no. 239. decennial. I.8.

NASHUA, NH, PMSA
> Census tracts. Report no. 95E. decennial. I.8.

NASHVILLE, TN, MSA
> Census tracts. Report no. 240. decennial. I.8.

NASSAU-SUFFOLK, NY, PMSA
> Census tracts. Report no. 245G. decennial. I.8.

NATIVE AMERICANS *see* INDIANS OF NORTH AMERICA

NEENAH, WI *see* APPLETON-OSHKOSH-NEENAH, WI, MSA

NEPAL
> Foreign economic trends. annual. II.9.

NETHERLANDS
> Foreign economic trends. semiannual. II.9.
> Foreign labor trends. annual. I.24.

NETHERLANDS ANTILLES
   Foreign economic trends. annual. II.9.
NEW BEDFORD, MA, MSA
   Census tracts. Report no. 241. decennial. I.8.
NEW BRITAIN, CT, PMSA
   Census tracts. Report no. 172D. decennial. I.8.
NEW HAVEN-MERIDEN, CT, MSA
   Census tracts. Report no. 242. decennial. I.8.
NEW LONDON-NORWICH, CT-RI, MSA
   Census tracts. Report no. 243. decennial. I.8.
NEW ORLEANS, LA, MSA
   Census tracts. Report no. 244. decennial. I.8.
NEW YORK, NY, PMSA
   Census tracts. Report no. 245H. decennial. I.8.
NEW YORK-NORTHERN NEW JERSEY-LONG ISLAND, NY-NJ-CT, CMSA
   Census tracts. Report nos. 245A-245L. decennial. I.8.
NEW ZEALAND
   Foreign economic trends. annual. II.9.
   Foreign labor trends. annual. I.24.
NEWARK, NJ, PMSA
   Census tracts. Report no. 245I. decennial. I.8.
NEWPORT NEWS, VA *see* NORFOLK-VIRGINIA BEACH-NEWPORT NEWS,
   VA, MSA
NIAGARA FALLS, NY, PMSA
   Census tracts. Report no. 100B. decennial. I.8.
NICARAGUA
   Foreign labor trends. annual. I.24.
NIGER
   Foreign economic trends. annual. II.9.
NIGERIA
   Foreign economic trends. annual. II.9.
   Foreign labor trends. annual. I.24.
NORFOLK-VIRGINIA BEACH-NEWPORT NEWS, VA, MSA
   Census tracts. Report no. 246. decennial. I.8.
NORMAL, IL *see* BLOOMINGTON-NORMAL, IL, MSA
NORWALK, CT, PMSA
   Census tracts. Report no. 245J. decennial. I.8.
NORWAY
   Foreign economic trends. annual. II.9.
   Foreign labor trends. annual. I.24.
NORWICH, CT *see* NEW LONDON-NORWICH, CT-RI, MSA

NURSES
>   Factbook: Health personnel, U.S. biennial. V.53.
>   *see also* HEALTH CARE

OAKLAND, CA, PMSA
>   Census tracts. Report no. 294A. decennial. I.8.

OCALA, FL, MSA
>   Census tracts. Report no. 247. decennial. I.8.

OCCUPATIONS
>   The American workforce: 1992-2005. biennial. III.3.
>   Career guide to industries. annual. III.2, V.19.
>   Census of population and housing. Equal employment opportunity file. decennial. IV.4, V.35.
>   Occupational employment in mining, construction, finance, and services. triennial. V.26.
>   Occupational outlook handbook. biennial. III.4, V.24.
>   Occupational outlook quarterly. quarterly. III.1, V.17.
>   Occupational projections and training data. biennial. III.5, V.25.
>   Occupations of federal white-collar and blue-collar workers. biennial. V.5.
>   *see also specific occupations, e.g.,* ENGINEERS; PHYSICIANS; SCIENTISTS*; and types of industries, e.g.,* EDUCATION; HEALTH CARE

OCEAN, NJ *see* MONMOUTH-OCEAN, NJ, PMSA

ODESSA, TX, MSA
>   Census tracts. Report no. 248. decennial. I.8.

OGDEN, UT *see* SALT LAKE CITY-OGDEN, UT, MSA

OKLAHOMA CITY, OK, MSA
>   Census tracts. Report no. 249. decennial. I.8.

OLYMPIA, WA, MSA
>   Census tracts. Report no. 250. decennial. I.8.

OMAHA, NE-IA, MSA
>   Census tracts. Report no. 251. decennial. I.8.

OMAN
>   Foreign economic trends. annual. II.9.

OPTOMETRISTS
>   Factbook: Health personnel, U.S. biennial. V.53.

ORANGE COUNTY, NY, PMSA
>   Census tracts. Report no. 245K. decennial. I.8.

OREM, UT, MSA *see* PROVO-OREM, UT, MSA

ORLANDO, FL, MSA
>   Census tracts. Report no. 252. decennial. I.8.

OSHKOSH, WI *see* APPLETON-OSHKOSH-NEENAH, WI, MSA

OSTEOPATHS
    Factbook: Health personnel, U.S. biennial. V.53.
OWENSBORO, KY, MSA
    Census tracts. Report no. 253. decennial. I.8.
OXNARD-VENTURA, CA, PMSA
    Census tracts. Report no. 215C. decennial. I.8.
PACIFIC ISLANDER AMERICANS *see* ASIAN AND PACIFIC ISLANDER
    AMERICANS
PAKISTAN
    Foreign economic trends. annual. II.9.
PALM BAY, FL *see* MELBOURNE-TITUSVILLE-PALM BAY, FL, MSA
PANAMA
    Foreign economic trends. annual. II.9.
    Foreign labor trends. annual. I.24.
PANAMA CITY, FL, MSA
    Census tracts. Report no. 254. decennial. I.8.
PAPUA-NEW GUINEA
    Foreign economic trends. annual. II.9.
PARAGUAY
    Foreign economic trends. annual. II.9.
PARKERSBURG-MARIETTA, WV-OH, MSA
    Census tracts. Report no. 255. decennial. I.8.
PASCAGOULA, MS, MSA
    Census tracts. Report no. 256. decennial. I.8.
PASCO, WA *see* RICHLAND-KENNEWICK-PASCO, WA, MSA
PASSAIC, NJ *see* BERGEN-PASSAIC, NJ, PMSA
PAWTUCKET-WOONSOCKET-ATTLEBORO, RI-MA, PMSA
    Census tracts. Report no. 269B. decennial. I.8.
PENSACOLA, FL, MSA
    Census tracts. Report no. 257. decennial. I.8.
PEORIA, IL, MSA
    Census tracts. Report no. 258. decennial. I.8.
PERU
    Foreign economic trends. annual. II.9.
    Foreign labor trends. annual. I.24.
PETALUMA, CA *see* SANTA ROSA-PETALUMA, CA, PMSA
PETERSBURG, VA *see* RICHMOND-PETERSBURG, VA, MSA
PHARMACISTS
    Factbook: Health personnel, U.S. biennial. V.53.
PHILADELPHIA, PA-NJ, PMSA
    Census tracts. Report no. 259A. decennial. I.8.

PHILADELPHIA-WILMINGTON-TRENTON, PA-NJ-DE-MD, CMSA
    Census tracts. Report nos. 259A-259D. decennial. I.8.
PHILIPPINES
    Foreign economic trends. semiannual. II.9.
    Foreign labor trends. annual. I.24.
PHOENIX, AZ, MSA
    Census tracts. Report no. 260. decennial. I.8.
PHYSICIANS
    Characteristics of physicians. irreg. V.65.
    Factbook: health personnel, U.S. biennial. V.53.
PINE BLUFF, AR, MSA
    Census tracts. Report no. 261. decennial. I.8.
PITTSBURGH, PA, PMSA
    Census tracts. Report no. 262B. decennial. I.8.
PITTSBURGH-BEAVER VALLEY, PA, CMSA
    Census tracts. Report nos. 262A-262B. decennial. I.8.
PITTSFIELD, MA, MSA
    Census tracts. Report no. 263. decennial. I.8.
PODIATRISTS
    Factbook: Health personnel, U.S. biennial. V.53.
POLAND
    Foreign economic trends. annual. II.9
POLICE *see* LAW ENFORCEMENT
POMPANO BEACH, FL *see* FORT LAUDERDALE-HOLLYWOOD-POMPANO
    BEACH, FL, PMSA
PONCE, PR, MSA
    Census tracts. Report no. 264. decennial. I.8.
PORTERVILLE, CA *see* VISALIA-TULARE-PORTERVILLE, CA, MSA
PORTLAND, ME, MSA
    Census tracts. Report no. 265. decennial. I.8.
PORTLAND, OR, PMSA
    Census tracts. Report no. 266A. decennial. I.8.
PORTLAND-VANCOUVER, OR-WA, CMSA
    Census tracts. Report nos. 266A-266B. decennial. I.8.
PORTSMOUTH-DOVER-ROCHESTER, NH-ME, MSA
    Census tracts. Report no. 267. decennial. I.8.
PORTUGAL
    Foreign economic trends. annual. II.9.
    Foreign labor trends. annual. I.24.
POSTAL SERVICE
    Annual report of the Postmaster General. annual. V.10.

POUGHKEEPSIE, NY, MSA
  Census tracts. Report no. 268. decennial. I.8.
PROVIDENCE, RI, PMSA
  Census tracts. Report no. 269C. decennial. I.8.
PROVIDENCE-PAWTUCKET-FALL RIVER, RI-MA, CMSA
  Census tracts. Report nos. 269A-269C. decennial. I.8.
PROVO-OREM, UT, MSA
  Census tracts. Report no. 270. decennial. I.8.
PSYCHOLOGISTS
  Factbook: Health personnel, U.S. biennial. V.53.
PUBLIC SECTOR see GOVERNMENT
PUBLIC UTILITIES
  Occupational employment in transportation, communications, utilities,
      and trade. irreg. V.36.
PUEBLO, CO, MSA
  Census tracts. Report no. 271. decennial. I.8.
QATAR
  Foreign economic trends. annual. II.9.
RACINE, WI, PMSA
  Census tracts. Report no. 231B. decennial. I.8.
RAILROADS
  Annual report. (U.S. Railroad Retirement Board). annual. V.66.
RALEIGH-DURHAM, NC, MSA
  Census tracts. Report no. 272. decennial. I.8.
RANTOUL, IL see CHAMPAIGN-URBANA-RANTOUL, IL, MSA
RAPID CITY, SD, MSA
  Census tracts. Report no. 273. decennial. I.8.
READING, PA, MSA
  Census tracts. Report no. 274. decennial. I.8.
REDDING, CA, MSA
  Census tracts. Report no. 275. decennial. I.8.
REFUGEES
  Refugee resettlement program; report to the Congress. annual. IV.30.
RENO, NV, MSA
  Census tracts. Report no. 276. decennial. I.8.
RETAIL TRADE
  Census of retail trade. Geographic area series. quinquennial. V.67.
  Occupational employment in transportation, communications,
      utilities, and trade. irreg. V.36.
RICHLAND-KENNEWICK-PASCO, WA, MSA
  Census tracts. Report no. 277. decennial. I.8.

RICHMOND-PETERSBURG, VA, MSA
 Census tracts. Report no. 278. decennial. I.8.
RIVERSIDE-SAN BERNARDINO, CA, PMSA
 Census tracts. Report no. 215D. decennial. I.8.
ROANOKE, VA, MSA
 Census tracts. Report no. 279. decennial. I.8.
ROCHESTER, MN, MSA
 Census tracts. Report no. 280. decennial. I.8.
ROCHESTER, NH *see* PORTSMOUTH-DOVER-ROCHESTER, NH-ME, MSA
ROCHESTER, NY, MSA
 Census tracts. Report no. 281. decennial. I.8.
ROCK HILL, SC *see* CHARLOTTE-GASTONIA-ROCK HILL, NC-SC, MSA
ROCK ISLAND, IL *see* DAVENPORT-ROCK ISLAND-MOLINE, IA-IL, MSA
ROCKFORD, IL, MSA
 Census tracts. Report no. 282. decennial. I.8.
ROMANIA
 Foreign economic trends. annual. II.9.
ROME, NY *see* UTICA-ROME, NY, MSA
RWANDA
 Foreign economic trends. annual. II.9.
SACRAMENTO, CA, MSA
 Census tracts. Report no. 283. decennial. I.8.
SAGINAW-BAY CITY-MIDLAND, MI, MSA
 Census tracts. Report no. 284. decennial. I.8.
ST. CLOUD, MN, MSA
 Census tracts. Report no. 285. decennial. I.8.
ST. JOSEPH, MO, MSA
 Census tracts. Report no. 286. decennial. I.8.
ST. LOUIS, MO-IL, MSA
 Census tracts. Report no. 287. decennial. I.8.
ST. LUCIA
 Foreign economic trends. annual. II.9
ST. PAUL, MN *see* MINNEAPOLIS-ST. PAUL, MN-WI, MSA
ST. PETERSBURG, FL *see* TAMPA-ST. PETERSBURG-CLEARWATER,
 FL, MSA
ST. VINCENT AND GRENADINES
 Foreign economic trends. annual. II.9.
SALEM, OR, MSA
 Census tracts. Report no. 288. decennial. I.8.

SALEM-GLOUCESTER, MA, PMSA
   Census tracts. Report no. 95F. decennial. I.8.
SALINAS-SEASIDE-MONTEREY, CA, MSA
   Census tracts. Report no. 289. decennial. I.8.
SALT LAKE CITY-OGDEN, UT, MSA
   Census tracts. Report no. 290. decennial. I.8.
SAN ANGELO, TX, MSA
   Census tracts. Report no. 291. decennial. I.8.
SAN ANTONIO, TX, MSA
   Census tracts. Report no. 292. decennial. I.8.
SAN BERNARDINO, CA *see* RIVERSIDE-SAN BERNARDINO, CA, PMSA
SAN DIEGO, CA, MSA
   Census tracts. Report no. 293. decennial. I.8.
SAN FRANCISCO, CA, PMSA
   Census tracts. Report no. 294B. decennial. I.8.
SAN FRANCISCO-OAKLAND-SAN JOSE, CA, CMSA
   Census tracts. Report nos. 294A-294F. decennial. I.8.
SAN JOSE, CA, PMSA
   Census tracts. Report no. 294C. decennial. I.8.
SAN JUAN, PR, PMSA
   Census tracts. Report no. 295B. decennial. I.8.
SAN JUAN-CAGUAS, PR, CMSA
   Census tracts. Report nos. 295A-295B. decennial. I.8.
SANTA ANA, CA *see* ANAHEIM-SANTA ANA, CA, PMSA
SANTA BARBARA-SANTA MARIA-LOMPOC, CA, MSA
   Census tracts. Report no. 296. decennial. I.8.
SANTA CRUZ, CA, PMSA
   Census tracts. Report no. 294D. decennial. I.8.
SANTA FE, NM, MSA
   Census tracts. Report no. 297. decennial. I.8.
SANTA MARIA, CA *see* SANTA BARBARA-SANTA MARIA-LOMPOC,
   CA, MSA
SANTA ROSA-PETALUMA, CA, PMSA
   Census tracts. Report no. 294E. decennial. I.8.
SARASOTA, FL, MSA
   Census tracts. Report no. 298. decennial. I.8.
SAUDI ARABIA
   Foreign economic trends. annual. II.9.
SAVANNAH, GA, MSA
   Census tracts. Report no. 299. decennial.
SCHENECTADY, NY *see* ALBANY-SCHENECTADY-TROY, NY, MSA

SCIENCE AND TECHNOLOGY
>International science and technology data update. annual. V.68.
>Science and engineering indicators. annual. V.70.
>Women and minorities in science and engineering. annual. V.72.

SCIENTISTS
>Characteristics of doctoral scientists and engineers in the U.S. biennial. V.69.
>International science and technology data update. annual. V.68.
>Scientists, engineers, and technicians in manufacturing industries: detailed statistical tables. triennial. V.89.
>Scientists, engineers, and technicians in nonmanufacturing industries: detailed statistical tables. triennial. V.73.
>Scientists, engineers, and technicians in trade and regulated industries. triennial. V.74.
>U.S. scientists and engineers. biennial. V.71.

SCRANTON-WILKES-BARRE, PA, MSA
>Census tracts. Report no. 300. decennial. I.8.

SEASIDE, CA *see* SALINAS-SEASIDE-MONTEREY, CA, MSA

SEATTLE, WA, PMSA
>Census tracts. Report no. 301A. decennial. I.8.

SEATTLE-TACOMA, WA, CMSA
>Census tracts. Report nos. 301A-301B. decennial. I.8.

SENEGAL
>Foreign economic trends. annual. II.9.
>Foreign labor trends. annual. I.24.

SERVICE INDUSTRIES
>Census of service industries. Geographic area series. quinquennial. V.75.
>Employment, hours, and earnings, United States, 1909-94. irreg. I.17
>Occupational employment in mining, construction, finance, and services. triennial. V.26.

SHARON, PA, MSA
>Census tracts. Report no. 302. decennial. I.8.

SHEBOYGAN, WI, MSA
>Census tracts. Report no. 303. decennial. I.8.

SHERMAN-DENISON, TX, MSA
>Census tracts. Report no. 304. decennial. I.8.

SHIPBUILDING
>Report on survey of U.S. shipbuilding and repair facilities. annual. V.76.

SHREVEPORT, LA, MSA
>Census tracts. Report no. 305. decennial. I.8.

SIERRA LEONE
>Foreign economic trends. annual. II.9.

SINGAPORE
>Foreign economic trends. annual. II.9.
>Foreign labor trends. annual. I.24.

SIOUX CITY, IA-NE, MSA
>Census tracts. Report no. 306. decennial. I.8.

SIOUX FALLS, SD, MSA
>Census tracts. Report no. 307. decennial. I.8.

SMALL BUSINESS
>The state of small business. annual. V.22.

SOMALIA
>Foreign economic trends. annual. II.9.

SOMERSET *see* MIDDLESEX-SOMERSET-HUNTERDON, NJ, PMSA

SOUTH AFRICA
>Foreign economic trends. annual. II.9.
>Foreign labor trends. annual. I.24.

SOUTH BEND-MISHAWAKA, IN, MSA
>Census tracts. Report no. 308. decennial. I.8.

SPAIN
>Foreign economic trends. semiannual. II.9.

SPARTANBURG, SC *see* GREENVILLE-SPARTANBURG, SC, MSA

SPOKANE, WA, MSA
>Census tracts. Report no. 309. decennial. I.8.

SPRINGDALE, AR *see* FAYETTEVILLE-SPRINGDALE, AR, MSA

SPRINGFIELD, IL, MSA
>Census tracts. Report no. 310. decennial. I.8.

SPRINGFIELD, MA, MSA
>Census tracts. Report no. 312. decennial. I.8.

SPRINGFIELD, MO, MSA
>Census tracts. Report no. 311. decennial. I.8.

SPRINGFIELD, OH *see* DAYTON-SPRINGFIELD, OH, MSA

SPRINGFIELD, OR *see* EUGENE-SPRINGFIELD, OR, MSA

SRI LANKA
>Foreign economic trends. annual. II.9.

STAMFORD, CT, PMSA
>Census tracts. Report no. 245L. decennial I.8.

STATE COLLEGE, PA, MSA
>Census tracts. Report no. 313. decennial. I.8.

STATE DATA *see* UNITED STATES—NATIONAL, STATES; *and other subdivisions under* UNITED STATES

STEEL INDUSTRY
> Quarterly report on the status of the steel industry. quarterly. V.96.

STEUBENVILLE-WEIRTON, OH-WV, MSA
> Census tracts. Report no. 314. decennial. I.8.

STOCKTON, CA, MSA
> Census tracts. Report no. 315. decennial. I.8.

STUDENTS
> School enrollment—social and economic characteristics of students. annual. IV.31.
> Youth indicators. irreg. IV.34.

SUDAN
> Foreign economic trends. annual. II.9.

SUFFOLK, NY *see* NASSAU-SUFFOLK, NY, PMSA

SURINAME
> Foreign economic trends. annual. II.9.
> Foreign labor trends. annual. I.24.

SWAZILAND
> Foreign economic trends. annual. II.9.

SWEDEN
> Foreign economic trends. annual. II.9.
> Foreign labor trends. annual. I.24.

SWITZERLAND
> Foreign economic trends. semiannual. II.9.
> Foreign labor trends. annual. I.24.

SYRACUSE, NY, MSA
> Census tracts. Report no. 316. decennial. I.8.

SYRIA
> Foreign economic trends. annual. II.9.

TACOMA, WA, PMSA
> Census tracts. Report no. 301B. decennial. I.8.

TAIWAN
> Foreign economic trends. semiannual. II.9.
> Foreign labor trends. annual. I.24.

TALLAHASSEE, FL, MSA
> Census tracts. Report no. 317. decennial. I.8.

TAMPA-ST. PETERSBURG-CLEARWATER, FL, MSA
> Census tracts. Report no. 318. decennial. I.8.

TANZANIA
> Foreign economic trends. annual. II.9.

TEACHERS *see* EDUCATION

TECHNOLOGY *see* SCIENCE AND TECHNOLOGY

TELECOMMUNICATIONS
>   Statistics of communications common carriers. annual. V.77.

TEMPLE, TX *see* KILLEEN-TEMPLE, TX, MSA

TERRE HAUTE, IN, MSA
>   Census tracts. Report no. 319. decennial. I.8.

TEXARKANA, TX-TEXARKANA, AR, MSA
>   Census tracts. Report no. 320. decennial. I.8.

TEXAS CITY, TX *see* GALVESTON-TEXAS CITY, TX, PMSA

THAILAND
>   Foreign economic trends. semiannual. II.9.
>   Foreign labor trends. annual. I.24.

THIBODAUX, LA *see* HOUMA-THIBODAUX, LA, MSA

TIMBER
>   Timber sales program. annual. V.78.

TITUSVILLE, TX *see* MELBOURNE-TITUSVILLE-PALM BAY, FL, MSA

TOGO
>   Foreign economic trends. annual. II.9.

TOLEDO, OH, MSA
>   Census tracts. Report no. 321. decennial. I.8.

TOPEKA, KS, MSA
>   Census tracts. Report no. 322. decennial. I.8.

TRADE UNION WORKERS
>   News. Union members. annual. IV.32.

TRANSPORTATION
>   Census of transportation. Geographic area series. Selected transportation
>   industries. quinquennial. V.80.
>   Census of transportation. Subject series. Selected transportation
>   industries. Miscellaneous subjects. quinquennial. V.81.
>   National transportation statistics. annual. V.79.
>   Occupational employment in transportation, communications,
>   utilities, and trade. irreg. V.36.

TRENTON, NJ, PMSA
>   Census tracts. Report no. 259B. decennial. I.8.

TRINIDAD AND TOBAGO
>   Foreign economic trends. annual. II.9.
>   Foreign labor trends. annual. I.24.

TROY, NY *see* ALBANY-SCHENECTADY-TROY, NY, MSA

TUCSON, AZ, MSA
>   Census tracts. Report no. 323. decennial. I.8.

TULARE, CA *see* VISALIA-TULARE-PORTERVILLE, CA, MSA

TULSA, OK, MSA
> Census tracts. Report no. 324. decennial. I.8.

TUNISIA
> Foreign economic trends. annual. II.9.
> Foreign labor trends. annual. I.24.

TURKEY
> Foreign economic trends. annual. II.9.
> Foreign labor trends. annual. I.24.

TUSCALOOSA, AL, MSA
> Census tracts. Report no. 325. decennial. I.8.

TYLER, TX, MSA
> Census tracts. Report no. 326. decennial. I.8.

UGANDA
> Foreign economic trends. annual. II.9.

UNEMPLOYMENT INSURANCE RECIPIENTS
> Unemployment insurance weekly claims report. weekly. IV.33.

UNIONS *see* TRADE UNIONS

UNITED ARAB EMIRATES
> Foreign economic trends. annual. II.9.

UNITED KINGDOM
> Foreign economic trends. semiannual. II.9.
> Foreign labor trends. annual. I.24.

UNITED STATES
> Business statistics. biennial. I.26.
> Commerce publications update. biweekly. II.1.
> Economic indicators. monthly. I.21.
> Economic report of the President. annual. I.23.
> Employment, hours, and earnings, United States. 1909-94. irreg. I.17.
> Employment, hours, and earnings, United States, 1981-93. irreg. I.18.
> Employment-unemployment: Hearings. monthly. II.2.
> Federal Reserve bulletin. monthly. II.3.
> Labor force statistics from Current Population Survey, 1948-87. irreg. I.20.
> Population profile of the United States. annual. I.25.
> Revised seasonally adjusted labor force statistics, 1978-87. irreg. II.7.
> Supplement to employment and earnings, revised establishment data. annual. I.6.
> Survey of current business. monthly. I.22.

UNITED STATES—CITIES/URBANIZED AREAS
> Social and economic characteristics. Urbanized areas. decennial. I.14.

UNITED STATES—CONGRESSIONAL DISTRICTS
> Population and housing characteristics for congressional districts.

VALLEJO-FAIRFIELD-NAPA, CA, PMSA
Census tracts. Report no. 294F. decennial. I.8.
VANCOUVER, WA, PMSA
Census tracts. Report no. 266B. decennial. I.8.
VENEZUELA
Foreign economic trends. semiannual. II.9.
VENTURA, CA *see* OXNARD-VENTURA, CA, PMSA
VETERANS
Affirmative employment statistics. biennial. V.3.
Reports to the Congress required by the Fair labor standards act.
annual. IV.3.
VICTORIA, TX, MSA
Census tracts. Report no. 328. decennial. I.8.
VINELAND-MILLVILLE-BRIDGETON, NJ, PMSA
Census tracts. Report no. 259C. decennial. I.8.
VIRGINIA BEACH *see* NORFOLK-VIRGINIA BEACH-NEWPORT NEWS,
VA, MSA
VISALIA-TULARE-PORTERVILLE, CA, MSA
Census tracts. Report no. 329. decennial. I.8.
WACO, TX, MSA
Census tracts. Report no. 330. decennial. I.8.
WARNER ROBINS, GA *see* MACON-WARNER ROBINS, GA, MSA
WARREN, OH *see* YOUNGSTOWN-WARREN, OH, MSA
WASHINGTON, DC-MD-VA, MSA
Census tracts. Report no. 331. decennial. I.8.
WATERBURY, CT, MSA
Census tracts. Report no. 332. decennial. I.8.
WATERLOO-CEDAR FALLS, IA, MSA
Census tracts. Report no. 333. decennial. I.8.
WAUSAU, WI, MSA
Census tracts. Report no. 334. decennial. I.8.
WEIRTON, WV *see* STEUBENVILLE-WEIRTON, OH-WV, MSA
WEST PALM BEACH-BOCA RATON-DELRAY BEACH, FL, MSA
Census tracts. Report no. 335. decennial. I.8.
WHEELING, WV-OH, MSA
Census tracts. Report no. 336. decennial. I.8.
WHITE-COLLAR WORKERS
Occupations of federal white-collar and blue-collar workers. V.5.
WHOLESALE TRADE
Census of wholesale trade. Geographic area series. quinquennial. V.82.
Census of wholesale trade. Subject series. Miscellaneous subjects.

YAKIMA, WA, MSA
    Census tracts. Report no. 342. decennial. I.8.
YEMEN ARAB REPUBLIC
    Foreign economic trends. annual. II.9.
YORK, PA, MSA
    Census tracts. Report no. 343. decennial. I.8.
YOUNGSTOWN-WARREN, OH, MSA
    Census tracts. Report no. 344. decennial. I.8.
YOUTH
    Youth indicators: trends in the well being of American youth. irreg.
        IV.34.
    Reports to the Congress required by the Fair labor standards act.
        annual. IV.3.
YUBA CITY, CA, MSA
    Census tracts. Report no. 345. decennial. I.8.
YUGOSLAVIA
    Foreign labor trends. annual. I.24.
YUMA, AZ, MSA
    Census tracts. Report no. 346. decennial. I.8.
ZAIRE
    Foreign economic trends. annual. II.9.
    Foreign labor trends. annual. I.24.
ZAMBIA
    Foreign economic trends. annual. II.9.
ZIMBABWE
    Foreign economic trends. annual. II.9.
    Foreign labor trends. annual. I.24.

Subject Index 2—
Income/Earnings

For income/earnings covering United States, the individual states, etc. *see* UNITED STATES; UNITED STATES—CONGRESSIONAL DISTRICTS; UNITED STATES—NATIONAL, STATES; *and other subject subdivisions of* UNITED STATES.

ALASKA
Occupational compensation survey. Summary. annual. VIII.13.
ALBANY, GA, MSA
Census tracts. Report no. 60. decennial. I.8.
Occupational compensation survey. Summary. annual. VIII.13.
ALBANY-SCHENECTADY-TROY, NY, MSA
Census tracts. Report no. 61. decennial. I.8.
Occupational compensation survey. Summary. annual. VIII.13.
ALBUQUERQUE, NM, MSA
Census tracts. Report no. 62. decennial. I.8.
Occupational compensation survey. Summary. annual. VIII.13.
ALEUTS
Census of population. Social and economic characteristics.
American Indian and Alaska native areas. decennial. VII.10.
ALEXANDRIA, LA, MSA
Census tracts. Report no. 63. decennial. I.8.
ALEXANDRIA-LEESVILLE AREA, LA
Occupational compensation survey. Summary. annual. VIII.13.
ALLENTOWN-BETHLEHEM-EASTON, PA-NJ, MSA
Census tracts. Report no. 64. decennial. I.8.
ALPENA-STANDISH-TAWAS CITY, MI, MSA
Occupational compensation survey. Summary. annual. VIII.13.
ALTOONA, PA, MSA
Census tracts. Report no. 65. decennial. I.8.
AMARILLO, TX, MSA
Census tracts. Report no. 66. decennial. I.8.
AMERICAN INDIANS *see* INDIANS OF NORTH AMERICA
ANAHEIM-SANTA ANA, CA, PMSA
Census tracts. Report no. 215A. decennial. I.8.
Occupational compensation survey. annual. VIII.11.
ANCESTRY
Census of population. Ancestry of the population in the United States.
decennial. VII.12.
ANCHORAGE, AK, MSA
Census tracts. Report no. 67. decennial. I.8.
ANDERSON, IN, MSA
Census tracts. Report no. 68. decennial. I.8.
ANDERSON, SC, MSA
Census tracts. Report no. 69. decennial. I.8.

ANN ARBOR, MI, PMSA
     Census tracts. Report no. 134A. decennial. I.8.
     Occupational compensation survey. Summary. annual. VIII.13.
ANNISTON, AL, MSA
     Census tracts. Report no. 70. decennial. I.8.
     Occupational compensation survey. Summary. annual. VIII.13.
APPLETON-OSHKOSH-NEENAH, WI, MSA
     Census tracts. Report no. 71. decennial. I.8.
     Occupational compensation survey. annual. VIII.11.
APPLIANCE REPAIR *see* REPAIRING INDUSTRY
ARECIBO, PR, MSA
     Census tracts. Report no. 72. decennial. I.8.
ARLINGTON, TX *see* FORT WORTH-ARLINGTON, TX, PMSA
ASHEVILLE, NC, MSA
     Census tracts. Report no. 73. decennial. I.8.
     Occupational compensation survey. Summary. annual. VIII.13.
ASHLAND, KY *see* HUNTINGTON-ASHLAND, WV-KY-OH, MSA
ASIA, EAST
     Foreign labor trends. annual. I.24.
ASIAN AND PACIFIC ISLANDER AMERICANS
     Asian and Pacific Islander population in the United States. Current
          population reports. irreg. VII.7.
     Census of population. Asians and Pacific Islanders in the United
          States. decennial. VII.4.
     We the American...Asians. decennial. VII.5.
     We the American...Pacific Islanders. decennial. VII.6.
ATHENS, GA, MSA
     Census tracts. Report no. 74. decennial. I.8.
ATLANTA, GA, MSA
     Census tracts. Report no. 75. decennial. I.8.
     Occupational compensation survey. annual. VIII.11.
ATLANTIC CITY, NJ, MSA
     Census tracts. Report no. 76. decennial. I.8.
     Occupational compensation survey. Summary. annual. VIII.13.
ATTLEBORO, MA *see* PAWTUCKET-WOONSOCKET-ATTLEBORO, RI-MA,
     PMSA
AUBURN, ME *see* LEWISTON-AUBURN, ME, MSA
AUGUSTA, GA-SC, MSA
     Census tracts. Report no. 77. decennial. I.8.
     Occupational compensation survey. annual. VIII.11.

AURORA-ELGIN, IL, PMSA
>Census tracts. Report no. 113A. decennial. I.8.

AUSTIN, TX, MSA
>Census tracts. Report no. 78. decennial. I.8.
>Occupational compensation survey. annual. VIII.11.
>Occupational compensation survey. Summary. annual. VIII.13.

AUSTRALIA
>Foreign labor trends. annual. I.24.

AUSTRIA
>Foreign labor trends. annual. I.24.

AUTOMOBILE INDUSTRY
>Auto dealer repair shops. irreg. VIII.20.
>Motor vehicles and parts. irreg. VIII.53.

BAKERSFIELD, CA, MSA
>Census tracts. Report no. 79. decennial. I.8.
>Occupational compensation survey. Summary. annual. VIII.13.

BALTIMORE, MD, MSA
>Census tracts. Report no. 80. decennial. I.8.
>Occupational compensation survey. annual. VIII.11.

BANGLADESH
>Foreign labor trends. annual. I.24.

BANGOR, ME, MSA
>Census tracts. Report no. 81. decennial. I.8.

BANKS AND BANKING
>Banking. irreg. VIII.21.

BATON ROUGE, LA, MSA
>Census tracts. Report no. 82. decennial. I.8.
>Occupational compensation survey. Summary. annual. VIII.13.

BATTLE CREEK, MI, MSA
>Census tracts. Report no. 83. decennial. I.8.
>Occupational compensation survey. Summary. annual. VIII.13.

BAY CITY, MI *see* SAGINAW-BAY CITY-MIDLAND, MI, MSA

BEAUMONT-PORT ARTHUR, TX, MSA
>Census tracts. Report no. 84. decennial. I.8.

BEAUMONT-PORT ARTHUR-ORANGE AND LAKE CHARLES, TX-LA, MSA
>(as defined by BLS)
>Occupational compensation survey. Summary. annual. VIII.13.

BEAVER COUNTY, PA, PMSA
>Census tracts. Report no. 262A. decennial. I.8.

BELGIUM
>Foreign labor trends. annual. I.24.

BELLINGHAM, WA, MSA
Census tracts. Report no. 85. decennial. I.8.
BELOIT, WI *see* JAMESVILLE-BELOIT, WI, MSA
BENTON HARBOR, MI, MSA
Census tracts. Report no. 86. decennial. I.8.
BERGEN-PASSAIC, NJ, PMSA
Census tracts. Report no. 245A. decennial. I.8.
Occupational compensation survey. annual. VIII.11.
BETHLEHEM, PA *see* ALLENTOWN-BETHLEHEM-EASTON, PA-NJ, MSA
BILLINGS, MT, MSA
Census tracts. Report no. 87. decennial. I.8.
Occupational compensation survey. annual. VIII.11.
BILOXI-GULFPORT, MS, MSA
Census tracts. Report no. 88. decennial. I.8.
BILOXI-GULFPORT AND PASCAGOULA, MS, MSA (as defined by BLS)
Occupational compensation survey. Summary. annual. VIII.13.
BINGHAMTON, NY, MSA
Census tracts. Report no. 89. decennial. I.8.
Occupational compensation survey. Summary. annual. VIII.13.
BIRMINGHAM, AL, MSA
Census tracts. Report no. 90. decennial. I.8.
Occupational compensation survey. Summary. annual. VIII.13.
BISMARK, ND, MSA
Census tracts. Report no. 91. decennial. I.8.
BLACK AMERICANS see AFRICAN-AMERICANS
BLOOMINGTON, IN, MSA
Census tracts. Report no. 92. decennial. I.8.
BLOOMINGTON-NORMAL, IL, MSA
Census tracts. Report no. 93. decennial. I.8.
BLOOMINGTON-VINCENNES AREA, IN
Occupational compensation survey. Summary. annual. VIII.13.
BLUE-COLLAR WORKERS
Occupations of federal white-collar and blue-collar workers. VIII.4.
BOCA RATON, FL *see* WEST PALM BEACH-BOCA RATON-DELRAY
BEACH, FL, MSA
BOISE CITY, ID, MSA
Census tracts. Report no. 94. decennial. I.8.
Occupational compensation survey. annual. VIII.11.
BOLIVIA
Foreign labor trends. annual. I.24.

BOSTON, MA, PMSA
> Census tracts. Report no. 95A. decennial. I.8.
> Occupational compensation survey. annual. VIII.11.

BOSTON-LAWRENCE-SALEM, MA-NH, CMSA
> Census tracts. Report nos. 95A-95F. decennial. I.8.

BOULDER-LONGMONT, CO, PMSA
> Census tracts. Report no. 132A. decennial. I.8.

BOX MANUFACTURING *see* PAPER BOX INDUSTRY

BRADENTON, FL, MSA
> Census tracts. Report no. 96. decennial. I.8.
> Occupational compensation survey. annual. VIII.11.

BRAZIL
> Foreign labor trends. annual. I.24.

BRAZORIA, TX, PMSA
> Census tracts. Report no. 176A. decennial. I.8.

BREMERTON, WA, MSA
> Census tracts. Report no. 97. decennial. I.8.

BREMERTON-SHELTON AREA, WA
> Occupational compensation survey. Summary. annual. VIII.13.

BRIDGEPORT-MILFORD, CT, PMSA
> Census tracts. Report no. 245B. decennial. I.8.

BRIDGETON, NJ *see* VINELAND-MILLVILLE-BRIDGETON, NJ, PMSA

BRISTOL, CT, PMSA
> Census tracts. Report no. 172A. decennial. I.8.

BRISTOL, VA *see* JOHNSON CITY-KINGSPORT-BRISTOL, TN-VA, MSA

BROCKTON, MA, PMSA
> Census tracts. Report no. 95B. decennial. I.8.

BROWNSVILLE-HARLINGEN, TX, MSA
> Census tracts. Report no. 98. decennial. I.8.

BRUNSWICK, GA, MSA
> Occupational compensation survey. Summary. annual. VIII.13.

BRYAN-COLLEGE STATION, TX, MSA
> Census tracts. Report no. 99. decennial. I.8.

BUFFALO, NY, MSA
> Occupational compensation survey. annual. VIII.11.

BUFFALO, NY, PMSA
> Census tracts. Report no. 100A. decennial. I.8.
> Occupational compensation survey. annual. VIII.11.

BUFFALO-NIAGARA FALLS, NY, CMSA
> Census tracts. Report nos. 100A-100B. decennial. I.8.

BURLINGTON, NC, MSA
Census tracts. Report no. 101. decennial. I.8.
BURLINGTON, VT, MSA
Census tracts. Report no. 102. decennial. I.8.
CAGUAS, PR, PMSA
Census tracts. Report no. 295A. decennial. I.8.
CANADA
Foreign labor trends. annual. I.24.
CANTON, OH, MSA
Census tracts. Report no. 103. decennial. I.8.
CAPE CORAL, FL *see* FORT MYERS-CAPE CORAL, FL MSA
CAREERS *see* OCCUPATIONS; *and specific occupations or careers, e.g.,*
ENGINEERS; PHYSICIANS; SCIENTISTS
CARIBBEAN, EASTERN
Foreign labor trends. annual. I.24.
CARLISLE, PA *see* HARRISBURG-LEBANON-CARLISLE, PA, MSA
CASPER, WY, MSA
Census tracts. Report no. 104. decennial. I.8.
CEDAR FALLS, IA *see* WATERLOO-CEDAR FALLS, IA, MSA
CEDAR RAPIDS, IA, MSA
Census tracts. Report no. 105. decennial. I.8.
Occupational compensation survey. Summary. annual. VIII.13.
CHAMPAIGN-URBANA-RANTOUL, IL, MSA
Census tracts. Report no. 106. decennial. I.8.
Occupational compensation survey. annual. VIII.11.
Occupational compensation survey. Summary. annual. VIII.13.
CHARLESTON, SC, MSA
Census tracts. Report no. 107. decennial. I.8.
Occupational compensation survey. annual. VIII.11.
Occupational compensation survey. Summary. annual. VIII.13.
CHARLESTON, WV, MSA
Census tracts. Report no. 108. decennial. I.8.
CHARLOTTE-GASTONIA-ROCK HILL, NC-SC, MSA
Census tracts. Report no. 109. decennial. I.8.
Occupational compensation survey. Summary. annual. VIII.13
CHARLOTTESVILLE, VA, MSA
Census tracts. Report no. 110. decennial. I.8.
CHATTANOOGA, TN-GA, MSA
Census tracts. Report no. 111. decennial. I.8.
Occupational compensation survey. Summary. annual. VIII.13.

CLEVELAND-AKRON-LORAIN, OH, CMSA
 Census tracts. Report nos. 117A-117C. decennial. I.8.
CLOTHING
 Men's and boys' shirts. irreg. VIII.57.
 Men's and boys' suits and coats. irreg. VIII.58.
 Women's and misses' dresses. irreg. VIII.59.
COAL MINING
 Bituminous coal mining. irreg. VIII.23.
COLLECTIVE BARGAINING
 Compensation and working conditions. monthly. VI.1.
COLLEGE STATION, TX *see* BRYAN-COLLEGE STATION, TX, MSA
COLOMBIA
 Foreign labor trends. annual. I.24.
COLORADO SPRINGS, CO, MSA
 Census tracts. Report no. 118. decennial. I.8.
COLUMBIA, MO, MSA
 Census tracts. Report no. 119. decennial. I.8.
COLUMBIA, SC, MSA
 Census tracts. Report no. 120. decennial. I.8.
COLUMBIA-SUMTER AREA, SC
 Occupational compensation survey. Summary. annual. VIII.13.
COLUMBUS, GA-AL, MSA
 Census tracts. Report no. 121. decennial. I.8.
 Occupational compensation survey. Summary. annual. VIII.13.
COLUMBUS, MS, MSA
 Occupational compensation survey. Summary. annual. VIII.13.
COLUMBUS, OH, MSA
 Census tracts. Report no. 122. decennial. I.8.
 Occupational compensation survey. annual. VIII.11.
COMPUTER SERVICE INDUSTRY
 Computer data and processing services. irreg. VIII.24.
CONNECTICUT
 Occupational compensation survey. Summary. annual. VIII.13.
CONSTRUCTION INDUSTRY
 Construction review. quarterly. VIII.25.
CORPUS CHRISTI, TX, MSA
 Census tracts. Report no. 123. decennial. I.8.
 Occupational compensation survey. annual. VIII.11.
COSTA RICA
 Foreign labor trends. annual. I.24.

COUNTIES *see* UNITED STATES—NATIONAL, STATES,
    COUNTIES/METROPOLITAN AREAS, CITIES; *and other subdivisions*
    under UNITED STATES; *also names of individual counties or*
    metropolitan areas, e.g., ABILENE, TX, MSA; BELLINGHAM, WA,
    MSA

CRIMINAL JUSTICE
    Sourcebook of criminal justice statistics. annual. VIII.26.

CUMBERLAND, MD-WV, MSA
    Census tracts. Report no. 124. decennial. I.8.

DALLAS, TX, PMSA
    Census tracts. Report no. 125A. decennial. I.8.

DALLAS-FORT WORTH, TX, CMSA
    Census tracts. Report nos. 125A-125B. decennial. I.8.

DALLAS-FORT WORTH, TX, MSA
    Occupational compensation survey. annual. VIII.11.

DANBURY, CT, MSA
    Occupational compensation survey. annual. VIII.11.

DANBURY, CT, PMSA
    Census tracts. Report no. 245C. decennial. I.8.

DANVILLE, VA, MSA
    Census tracts. Report no. 126. decennial. I.8.

DAVENPORT-ROCK ISLAND-MOLINE, IA-IL, MSA
    Census tracts. Report no. 127. decennial. I.8.
    Occupational compensation survey. annual. VIII.11.

DAYTON-SPRINGFIELD, OH, MSA
    Census tracts. Report no. 128. decennial. I.8.
    Occupational compensation survey. Summary. annual. VIII.13.

DAYTONA BEACH, FL, MSA
    Census tracts. Report no. 129. decennial. I.8.
    Occupational compensation survey. Summary. annual. VIII.13.

DECATUR, AL, MSA
    Census tracts. Report no. 130. decennial. I.8.

DECATUR, IL, MSA
    Census tracts. Report no. 131. decennial. I.8.
    Occupational compensation survey. annual. VIII.11.
    Occupational compensation survey. Summary. annual. VIII.13.

DELRAY BEACH *see* WEST PALM BEACH-BOCA RATON-DELRAY BEACH,
    FL, MSA

DENISON, TX *see* SHERMAN-DENISON, TX, MSA

DENMARK
    Foreign labor trends. annual. I.24.

DENVER, CO, PMSA
  Census tracts. Report no. 132B. decennial. I.8.
DENVER-BOULDER, CO, CMSA
  Census tracts. Report nos. 132A-132B. decennial. I.8.
DENVER-BOULDER, CO, MSA (as defined by BLS)
  Occupational compensation survey. annual. VIII.11.
DEPARTMENT STORES
  Department stores. irreg. VIII.27.
DES MOINES, IA, MSA
  Census tracts. Report no. 133. decennial. I.8.
  Occupational compensation survey. Summary. annual. VIII.13.
DETROIT, MI, PMSA
  Census tracts. Report no. 134B. decennial. I.8.
  Occupational compensation survey. annual. VIII.11.
DETROIT-ANN ARBOR, MI, CMSA
  Census tracts. Report nos. 134A-134B. decennial. I.8.
DISABLED
  Annual report on the employment of minorities, women, and people with
    disabilities in the federal government. annual. VIII.1.
  Chartbook on work disability in the United States. irreg. VII.23.
  Labor force status and other characteristics of persons with a work
    disability. irreg. VII.24.
  OASDI beneficiaries by state and county. annual. VII.31.
  SSI recipients by state and county. annual. VII.33.
DOMINICAN REPUBLIC
  Foreign labor trends. annual. I.24.
DOTHAN, AL, MSA
  Census tracts. Report no. 135. decennial. I.8.
  Occupational compensation survey. Summary. annual. VIII.13.
DOVER, NH see PORTSMOUTH-DOVER-ROCHESTER, NH-ME, MSA
DUBUQUE, IA, MSA
  Census tracts. Report no. 136. decennial. I.8.
DULUTH, MN-WI, MSA
  Census tracts. Report no. 137. decennial. I.8.
  Occupational compensation survey. Summary. annual. VIII.13.
DUNKIRK, NY see JAMESTOWN-DUNKIRK, NY, MSA
DURHAM, NC see RALEIGH-DURHAM, NC, MSA
EASTERN CARIBBEAN
  Foreign labor trends. annual. I.24.
EASTON, PA see ALLENTOWN-BETHLEHEM-EASTON, PA-NJ, MSA

EAU CLAIRE, WI, MSA
> Census tracts. Report no. 138. decennial. I.8.

ECUADOR
> Foreign labor trends. annual. I.24.

EDINBURG, TX *see* McCALLEN-EDINBURG-MISSION, TX, MSA

EDUCATION
> Condition of education. annual. VIII.28.
> Digest of education statistics. annual. VIII.29.
> Salaries of full-time instructional faculty on 9- and 10-month contracts in institutions of higher education. annual. VIII.30.
> State higher education profiles. annual. VIII.31.
> State profiles of public elementary and secondary education. biennial. VIII.32.

EDUCATIONAL STATUS
> Census of population. Education in the United States. decennial. VII.26.
> Digest of education statistics. annual. VIII.29.
> Educational attainment in the United States. annual. VII.25.
> What's it worth? irreg. VII.27.

EGYPT
> Foreign labor trends. annual. I.24.

EL PASO, TX, MSA
> Census tracts. Report no. 139. decennial. I.8.

EL PASO-ALAMOGORDO-LAS CRUCES, TX-NM, MSA
> Occupational compensation survey. Summary. annual. VIII.13.

EL SALVADOR
> Foreign labor trends. annual. I.24.

ELECTRIC INDUSTRY
> Electric and gas utilities. irreg. VIII.33.

ELGIN, IL *see* AURORA-ELGIN, IL, PMSA

ELKHART-GOSHEN, IN, MSA
> Census tracts. Report no. 140. decennial. I.8.
> Occupational compensation survey. annual. VIII.11.

ELMIRA, NY, MSA
> Census tracts. Report no. 141. decennial. I.8.

ELYRIA, OH *see* LORAIN-ELYRIA, OH, PMSA

ENGINEERING
> Science and engineering indicators. biennial. VIII.45
> Women and minorities in science and engineering. biennial. VIII.46.

ENGINEERS
> Characteristics of doctoral scientists and engineers in the U.S. biennial. VIII.44.

ENID, OK, MSA
      Census tracts. Report no. 142. decennial. I.8.
ERIE, PA, MSA
      Census tracts. Report no. 143. decennial. I.8.
ESKIMOS
      Census of population. Social and economic characteristics. American
            Indian and Alaska native areas. decennial. VII.10.
EUGENE-SPRINGFIELD, OR, MSA
      Census tracts. Report no. 144. decennial. I.8.
EUGENE-SPRINGFIELD-MEDFORD-ROSEBURG-KLAMATH FALLS-
      GRANTS
      PASS AREA, OR
      Occupational compensation survey. Summary. annual. VIII.13.
EUROPE, EASTERN
      Foreign labor trends. annual. I.24.
EVANSVILLE, IN-KY, MSA
      Census tracts. Report no. 145. decennial. I.8.
EXECUTIVES
      White-collar pay: private goods-producing industries. biennial.
            VIII.52.
      White-collar pay: private service-producing industries. biennial.
            VIII.47.
FAIRFIELD, CA *see* VALLEJO-FAIRFIELD-NAPA, CA, PMSA
FALL RIVER, MA-RI, PMSA
      Census tracts. Report no. 269A. decennial. I.8.
FARGO-MOORHEAD, ND-MN, MSA
      Census tracts. Report no. 146. decennial. I.8.
FAYETTE, KY *see* LEXINGTON-FAYETTE, KY, MSA
FAYETTEVILLE, NC, MSA
      Census tracts. Report no. 147. decennial. I.8.
      Occupational compensation survey. Summary. annual. VIII.13.
FAYETTEVILLE-SPRINGDALE, AR, MSA
      Census tracts. Report no. 148. decennial. I.8.
FINLAND
      Foreign labor trends. annual. I.24.
FITCHBURG-LEOMINSTER, MA, MSA
      Census tracts. Report no. 149. decennial. I.8.
FLINT, MI, MSA
      Census tracts. Report no. 150. decennial. I.8.
FLORENCE, AL, MSA
      Census tracts. Report no. 151. decennial. I.8.

FLORENCE, SC, MSA
> Census tracts. Report no. 152. decennial. I.8.
> Occupational compensation survey. annual. VIII.11.

FLORIDA, NORTHWESTERN
> Occupational compensation survey. Summary. annual. VIII.13.

FLOUR MILLS
> Grain mill products. irreg. VIII.60.

FOREIGN BORN
> Census of population. The foreign population in the United States. decennial. VII.13.
> We the American…foreign born. decennial. VII.14.

FOREIGN COUNTRIES
> Economic report of the President. annual. I.23.
> Foreign labor trends. annual. I.24.
> Handbook of labor statistics. irreg. I.19.
> International comparisons of hourly compensation costs for production workers in manufacturing. semiannual. VIII.51.
> *see also names of specific countries, e.g.,* AUSTRALIA, DENMARK, etc.

FORT COLLINS-LOVELAND, CO, MSA
> Census tracts. Report no. 153. decennial. I.8.

FORT LAUDERDALE-HOLLYWOOD-POMPANO BEACH, FL, PMSA
> Census tracts. Report no. 229A. decennial. I.8.
> Occupational compensation survey. Summary. annual. VIII.13.

FORT MYERS-CAPE CORAL, FL, MSA
> Census tracts. Report no. 154. decennial. I.8.

FORT PIERCE, FL, MSA
> Census tracts. Report no. 155. decennial. I.8.

FORT SMITH, AR-OK, MSA
> Census tracts. Report no. 156. decennial. I.8.
> Occupational compensation survey. Summary. annual. VIII.13.

FORT WALTON BEACH, FL, MSA
> Census tracts. Report no. 157. decennial. I.8.

FORT WAYNE, IN, MSA
> Census tracts. Report no. 158. decennial. I.8.
> Occupational compensation survey. Summary. annual. VIII.13.

FORT WORTH-ARLINGTON, TX, PMSA
> Census tracts. Report no. 125B. decennial. I.8.

FOUNDRIES
> Iron and steel foundries. irreg. VIII.75.

FRANCE
> Foreign labor trends. annual. I.24.

FRESNO, CA, MSA
> Census tracts. Report no. 159. decennial. I.8.
> Occupational compensation survey. annual. VIII.11.

FURNITURE INDUSTRY
> Wood household furniture. irreg. VIII.61.

GADSDEN, AL, MSA
> Census tracts. Report no. 160. decennial. I.8.
> Occupational compensation survey. Summary. annual. VIII.13.

GAINESVILLE, FL, MSA
> Census tracts. Report no. 161. decennial. I.8.
> Occupational compensation survey. annual. VIII.11.

GALVESTON-TEXAS CITY, TX, PMSA
> Census tracts. Report no. 176B. decennial. I.8.

GARY-HAMMOND, IN, PMSA
> Census tracts. Report no. 113C. decennial. I.8.
> Occupational compensation survey. annual. VIII.11.

GAS INDUSTRY
> Electric and gas utilities. irreg. VIII.33.
> Oil and gas extraction. irreg. VIII.34.

GASTONIA, NC *see* CHARLOTTE-GASTONIA-ROCK HILL, NC-SC, MSA

GERMANY
> Foreign labor trends. annual. I.24.

GHANA
> Foreign labor trends. annual. I.24.

GLASS MANUFACTURE
> Pressed or blown glass and glassware. irreg. VIII.62.

GLENS FALLS, NY, MSA
> Census tracts. Report no. 162. decennial. I.8.

GLOUCESTER, MA *see* SALEM-GLOUCESTER, MA, PMSA

GOLDSBORO, NC, MSA
> Occupational compensation survey. Summary. annual. VIII.13.

GOSHEN, IN, MSA *see* ELKHART-GOSHEN, IN, MSA

GOVERNMENT—COUNTY
> County government employment. annual. VIII.6.

GOVERNMENT—FEDERAL
> Annual report on the employment of minorities, women, and people with disabilities in the federal government. annual. VIII.1.
> Occupations of federal white-collar and blue-collar workers. biennial. VIII.4.

Pay structure of the federal civil service. annual. VIII.2.

Salary tables [for] executive branch of the government. annual. VIII.3.

GOVERNMENT—LOCAL

City employment. annual. VIII.5.

GOVERNMENT—STATE, LOCAL

Census of governments. Public employment. quinquennial. VIII.9.

Job patterns for minorities and women in state and local government. annual. VIII.7.

Public employment. annual. VIII.8.

GRAIN MILLS *see* FLOUR MILLS

GRAND FORKS, ND, MSA

Census tracts. Report no. 163. decennial. I.8.

GRAND ISLAND-HASTINGS, NE, MSA

Occupational compensation survey. Summary. annual. VIII.13.

GRAND RAPIDS, MI, MSA

Census tracts. Report no. 164. decennial. I.8.

GREAT FALLS, MT, MSA

Census tracts. Report no. 165. decennial. I.8.

GREECE

Foreign labor trends. annual. I.24.

GREELEY, CO, MSA

Census tracts. Report no. 166. decennial. I.8.

GREEN BAY, WI, MSA

Census tracts. Report no. 167. decennial. I.8.

Occupational compensation survey. Summary. annual. VIII.13.

GREENSBORO-WINSTON SALEM-HIGH POINT, NC, MSA

Census tracts. Report no. 168. decennial. I.8.

Occupational compensation survey. Summary. annual. VIII.13.

GREENVILLE-SPARTANBURG, SC, MSA

Census tracts. Report no. 169. decennial. I.8.

Occupational compensation survey. Summary. annual. VIII.13.

GULFPORT, MS *see* BILOXI-GULFPORT, MS, MSA

GUYANA

Foreign labor trends. annual. I.24.

HAGERSTOWN-CUMBERLAND-CHAMBERSBURG, MD-PA-WV

Occupational compensation survey. Summary. annual. VIII.13.

HAGERSTOWN, MD, MSA

Census tracts. Report no. 170. decennial. I.8.

HAITI

Foreign labor trends. annual. I.24.

HOTELS
>Hotels and motels. irreg. VIII.37.

HOUMA-THIBODAUX, LA, MSA
>Census tracts. Report no. 175. decennial. I.8.

HOUSTON, TX, PMSA
>Census tracts. Report no. 176C. decennial. I.8.
>Occupational compensation survey. annual. VIII.11.

HOUSTON-GALVESTON-BRAZORIA, TX, CMSA
>Census tracts. Report nos. 176A-176C. decennial. I.8.

HUNTERDON, NJ *see* MIDDLESEX-SOMERSET-HUNTERDON, NJ, PMSA

HUNTINGTON-ASHLAND, WV-KY-OH, MSA
>Census tracts. Report no. 177. decennial. I.8.

HUNTSVILLE, AL, MSA
>Census tracts. Report no. 178. decennial. I.8.
>Occupational compensation survey. annual. VIII.11.

ICELAND
>Foreign labor trends. annual. I.24.

INDIA
>Foreign labor trends. annual. I.24.

INDIANAPOLIS, IN, MSA
>Census tracts. Report no. 179. decennial. I.8.
>Occupational compensation survey. annual. VIII.11.

INDIANS OF NORTH AMERICA
>Census of population. Characteristics of American Indians by tribe and language. decennial. VII.9B.
>Census of population. Social and economic characteristics. American Indian and Alaska Native areas. decennial. VII.10.
>We the first Americans. decennial. VII.11.

INDONESIA
>Foreign labor trends. annual. I.24.

INDUSTRIAL RELATIONS
>Compensation and working conditions. monthly. VI.1.

INDUSTRIES
>BEA regional projections to 2040. quinquennial. VIII.16.
>Career guide to industries. annual. VIII.10A.
>U.S. industrial outlook. annual. VIII.14.
>*see also specific industries, e.g.,* CONSTRUCTION INDUSTRY; MANUFACTURING; PAPER INDUSTRY

INSURANCE
>Life and health insurance carriers. irreg. VIII.38.

INTERNATIONAL LABOR ACTIVITIES
>Foreign labor trends. annual. I.24.

JOPLIN, MO, MSA
>   Census tracts. Report no. 190. decennial. I.8.

JORDAN
>   Foreign labor trends. annual. I.24.

JUSTICE *see* CRIMINAL JUSTICE; LAW ENFORCEMENT

KALAMAZOO, MI, MSA
>   Census tracts. Report no. 191. decennial. I.8.

KANKAKEE, IL, MSA
>   Census tracts. Report no. 192. decennial. I.8.

KANSAS CITY, MO-KS, MSA
>   Census tracts. Report no. 193. decennial. I.8.
>   Occupational compensation survey. annual. VIII.11.

KENNEWICK, WA *see* RICHLAND-KENNEWICK-PASCO, WA, MSA

KENOSHA, WI, PMSA
>   Census tracts. Report no. 113E. decennial. I.8.

KENYA
>   Foreign labor trends. annual. I.24.

KILLEEN-TEMPLE, TX, MSA
>   Census tracts. Report no. 194. decennial. I.8.

KINGSPORT, TN *see* JOHNSON CITY-KINGSPORT-BRISTOL,
>   TN-VA, MSA

KNOXVILLE, TN, MSA
>   Census tracts. Report no. 195. decennial. I.8.
>   Occupational compensation survey. Summary. annual. VIII.13.

KOKOMO, IN, MSA
>   Census tracts. Report no. 196. decennial. I.8.
>   Occupational compensation survey. annual. VIII.11.

KOREA
>   Foreign labor trends. annual. I.24.

KUWAIT
>   Foreign labor trends. annual. I.24.

LA CROSSE, WI, MSA
>   Census tracts. Report no. 197. decennial. I.8.

LA CROSSE-SPARTA, WI, MSA
>   Occupational compensation survey. Summary. annual. VIII.13.

LAFAYETTE, LA, MSA
>   Census tracts. Report no. 198. decennial. I.8.

LAFAYETTE-WEST LAFAYETTE, IN, MSA
>   Census tracts. Report no. 199. decennial. I.8.

LAKE CHARLES, LA, MSA
>   Census tracts. Report no. 200. decennial. I.8.

LAKE COUNTY, IL, PMSA
    Census tracts. Report no. 113F. decennial. I.8.
LAKELAND-WINTER HAVEN, FL, MSA
    Census tracts. Report no. 201. decennial. I.8.
LANCASTER, PA, MSA
    Census tracts. Report no. 202. decennial. I.8.
LANSING-EAST LANSING, MI, MSA
    Census tracts. Report no. 203. decennial. I.8.
LAREDO, TX, MSA
    Census tracts. Report no. 204. decennial. I.8.
    Occupational compensation survey. Summary. annual. VIII.13.
LAS CRUCES, NM, MSA
    Census tracts. Report no. 205. decennial. I.8.
LAS VEGAS, NV, MSA
    Census tracts. Report no. 206. decennial. I.8.
LAS VEGAS-TENOPAH, NV, MSA (as defined by BLS)
    Occupational compensation survey. Summary. annual. VIII.13.
LATIN AMERICA
    Foreign labor trends. annual. I.24.
LATIN AMERICANS *see* HISPANICS
LAW ENFORCEMENT
    Profiles of state and local law enforcement agencies. irreg. VIII.40.
    Sheriffs' departments. triennial. VIII.39.
LAWRENCE, KS, MSA
    Census tracts. Report no. 207. decennial. I.8.
LAWRENCE-HAVERHILL, MA-NH, PMSA
    Census tracts. Report no. 95C. decennial. I.8.
    Occupational compensation survey. annual. VIII.11.
LAWTON, OK, MSA
    Census tracts. Report no. 208. decennial. I.8.
LEBANON, PA *see* HARRISBURG-LEBANON-CARLISLE, PA, MSA
LEOMINSTER, MA *see* FITCHBURG-LEOMINSTER, MA, MSA
LEWISTON-AUBURN, ME, MSA
    Census tracts. Report no. 209. decennial. I.8.
LEXINGTON-FAYETTE, KY, MSA
    Census tracts. Report no. 210. decennial. I.8.
    Occupational compensation survey. Summary. annual. VIII.13.
LIBERIA
    Foreign labor trends. annual. I.24.

LIMA, OH, MSA
>Census tracts. Report no. 211. decennial. I.8.
>Occupational compensation survey. Summary. annual. VIII.13.

LINCOLN, NE, MSA
>Census tracts. Report no. 212. decennial. I.8.

LITTLE ROCK-NORTH LITTLE ROCK, AR, MSA
>Census tracts. Report no. 213. decennial. I.8.
>Occupational compensation survey. annual. VIII.11.

LOGANSPORT-PERU, IN, MSA
>Occupational compensation survey. Summary. annual. VIII.13.

LOMPOC, CA *see* SANTA BARBARA-SANTA MARIA-LOMPOC, CA, MSA

LONG BEACH, CA *see* LOS ANGELES-LONG BEACH, CA, PMSA

LONGMONT, CO *see* BOULDER-LONGMONT, CO, PMSA

LONGVIEW-MARSHALL, TX, MSA
>Census tracts. Report no. 214. decennial. I.8.
>Occupational compensation survey. annual. VIII.11.

LORAIN-ELYRIA, OH, PMSA
>Census tracts. Report no. 117C. decennial. I.8.
>Occupational compensation survey. Summary. annual. VIII.13.

LOS ANGELES-ANAHEIM-RIVERSIDE, CA, CMSA
>Census tracts. Report nos. 215A-215D. decennial. I.8.

LOS ANGELES-LONG BEACH, CA, PMSA
>Census tracts. Report no. 215B. decennial. I.8.
>Occupational compensation survey. annual. VIII.11.

LOUISVILLE, KY-IN, MSA
>Census tracts. Report no. 216. decennial. I.8.
>Occupational compensation survey. annual. VIII.11.

LOVELAND, CO *see* FORT COLLINS-LOVELAND, CO, MSA

LOWELL, MA-NH, PMSA
>Census tracts. Report no. 95D. decennial. I.8.

LOWER EASTERN SHORE, MD-VA-DE, MSA
>Occupational compensation survey. Summary. annual. VIII.13.

LUBBOCK, TX, MSA
>Census tracts. Report no. 217. decennial. I.8.

LYNCHBURG, VA, MSA
>Census tracts. Report no. 218. decennial. I.8.

MACON-WARNER ROBINS, GA, MSA
>Census tracts. Report no. 219. decennial. I.8.
>Occupational compensation survey. Summary. annual. VIII.13.

MELBOURNE-TITUSVILLE-PALM BAY, FL, MSA
>Census tracts. Report no. 226. decennial. I.8.
>Occupational compensation survey. Summary. annual. VIII.13.

MEMPHIS, TN-AR-MS, MSA
>Census tracts. Report no. 227. decennial. I.8.
>Occupational compensation survey. annual. VIII.11.

MERCED, CA, MSA
>Census tracts. Report no. 228. decennial. I.8.

MERIDEN *see* NEW HAVEN-MERIDEN, CT, MSA

MERIDIAN, MS, MSA
>Occupational compensation survey. Summary. annual. VIII.13.

METALWORKING MACHINERY
>Metalworking machinery manufacturing. irreg. VIII.65.

MEXICAN-AMERICANS *see* HISPANIC AMERICANS

MEXICO
>Foreign labor trends. annual. I.24.

MIAMI-FORT LAUDERDALE, FL, CMSA
>Census tracts. Report nos. 229A-229B. decennial. I.8.

MIAMI-HIALEAH, FL, PMSA
>Census tracts. Report no. 229B. decennial. I.8.
>Occupational compensation survey. annual. VIII.11.

MIDDLESEX-SOMERSET-HUNTERDON, NJ, PMSA
>Census tracts. Report no. 245E. decennial. I.8.
>Occupational compensation survey. annual. VIII.11.

MIDDLETOWN, CT, PMSA
>Census tracts. Report no. 172C. decennial. I.8.

MIDDLETOWN, OH *see* HAMILTON-MIDDLETOWN, OH, PMSA

MIDLAND, MI *see* SAGINAW-BAY CITY-MIDLAND, MI, MSA

MIDLAND, TX, MSA
>Census tracts. Report no. 230. decennial. I.8.

MILFORD, CT *see* BRIDGEPORT-MILFORD, CT, PMSA

MILLVILLE, NJ *see* VINELAND-MILLVILLE-BRIDGETON, NJ, PMSA

MILLWORK INDUSTRY
>Millwork. irreg. VIII.66.

MILWAUKEE, WI, PMSA
>Census tracts. Report no. 231A. decennial. I.8.
>Occupational compensation survey. annual. VIII.11.

MILWAUKEE-RACINE, WI, CMSA
>Census tracts. Report nos. 231A-231B. decennial. I.8.

MINERAL INDUSTRY
>Minerals yearbook. annual. VIII.41.

MINNEAPOLIS-ST. PAUL, MN-WI, MSA
>Census tracts. Report no. 232. decennial. I.8.
>Occupational compensation survey. annual. VIII.11.

MINORITIES
>Annual report on the employment of minorities, women, and people with disabilities in the federal government. annual VIII.1.
>Job patterns for minorities and women in state and local government. annual. VIII.7.
>Women and minorities in science and engineering. biennial. VIII.46.
>*see also specific minorities, e.g.,* AFRICAN-AMERICANS; ASIAN AND PACIFIC ISLANDER AMERICANS; HISPANIC AMERICANS; etc.

MISHAWAKA, IN *see* SOUTH BEND-MISHAWAKA, IN, MSA

MISSION, TX *see* McALLEN-EDINBURG-MISSION, TX, MSA

MOBILE, AL, MSA
>Census tracts. Report no. 233. decennial. I.8.
>Occupational compensation survey. annual. VIII.11.
>Occupational compensation survey. Summary. annual. VIII.13.

MODESTO, CA, MSA
>Census tracts. Report no. 234. decennial. I.8.

MOLINE, IL *see* DAVENPORT-ROCK ISLAND-MOLINE, IA-IL, MSA

MONMOUTH-OCEAN, NJ, PMSA
>Census tracts. Report no. 245F. decennial. I.8.
>Occupational compensation survey. annual. VIII.11.

MONROE, LA, MSA
>Census tracts. Report no. 235. decennial. I.8.

MONTANA
>Occupational compensation survey. Summary. annual. VIII.13.

MONTEREY, CA *see* SALINAS-SEASIDE-MONTEREY, CA, MSA

MONTGOMERY, AL, MSA
>Census tracts. Report no. 236. decennial. I.8.
>Occupational compensation survey. Summary. annual. VIII.13.

MOORHEAD, MN *see* FARGO-MOORHEAD, ND-MN, MSA

MORGANTOWN, NC *see* HICKORY-MORGANTOWN, NC, MSA

MOROCCO
>Foreign labor trends. annual. I.24.

MUNCIE, IN, MSA
>Census tracts. Report no. 237. decennial. I.8.

MUSKEGON, MI, MSA
>Census tracts. Report no. 238. decennial. I.8.

NAPA, CA *see* VALLEJO-FAIRFIELD-NAPA, CA, PMSA

NAPLES, FL, MSA
    Census tracts. Report no. 239. decennial. I.8.
NASHUA, NH, PMSA
    Census tracts. Report no. 95E. decennial. I.8.
NASHVILLE, TN, MSA
    Census tracts. Report no. 240. decennial. I.8.
    Occupational compensation survey. annual. VIII.11.
NASSAU-SUFFOLK, NY, PMSA
    Census tracts. Report no. 245G. decennial. I.8.
    Occupational compensation survey. annual. VIII.11.
NATIVE AMERICANS *see* INDIANS OF NORTH AMERICA
NEENAH, WI *see* APPLETON-OSHKOSH-NEENAH, WI, MSA
NETHERLANDS
    Foreign labor trends. annual. I.24.
NEW BEDFORD, MA, MSA
    Census tracts. Report no. 241. decennial. I.8.
NEW BRITAIN, CT, PMSA
    Census tracts. Report no. 172D. decennial. I.8.
NEW HAVEN-MERIDEN, CT, MSA
    Census tracts. Report no. 242. decennial. I.8.
NEW LONDON-NORWICH, CT-RI, MSA
    Census tracts. Report no. 243. decennial. I.8.
NEW ORLEANS, LA, MSA
    Census tracts. Report no. 244. decennial. I.8.
    Occupational compensation survey. annual. VIII.11.
NEW YORK, NORTHERN
    Occupational compensation survey. Summary. annual. VIII.13.
NEW YORK, NY, PMSA
    Census tracts. Report no. 245H. decennial. I.8.
    Occupational compensation survey. annual. VIII.11.
NEW YORK-NORTHERN NEW JERSEY-LONG ISLAND, NY-NJ-CT, CMSA
    Census tracts. Report nos. 245A-245L. decennial. I.8.
NEW ZEALAND
    Foreign labor trends. annual. I.24.
NEWARK, NJ, PMSA
    Census tracts. Report no. 245I. decennial. I.8.
    Occupational compensation survey. annual. VIII.11.
NEWPORT NEWS, VA *see* NORFOLK-VIRGINIA BEACH-NEWPORT NEWS,
    VA, MSA
NIAGARA FALLS, NY, PMSA
    Census tracts. Report no. 100B. decennial. I.8.

NICARAGUA
>   Foreign labor trends. annual. I.24.

NIGERIA
>   Foreign labor trends. annual. I.24.

NORFOLK-VIRGINIA BEACH-NEWPORT NEWS, VA, MSA
>   Census tracts. Report no. 246. decennial. I.8.
>   Occupational compensation survey. Summary. annual. VIII.13.

NORMAL, IL *see* BLOOMINGTON-NORMAL, IL, MSA

NORTH DAKOTA
>   Occupational compensation survey. Summary. annual. VIII.13.

NORWALK, CT, PMSA
>   Census tracts. Report no. 245J. decennial. I.8.

NORWAY
>   Foreign labor trends. annual. I.24.

NORWICH, CT *see* NEW LONDON-NORWICH, CT-RI, MSA

NURSES *see* HEALTH CARE; HOSPITALS; NURSING HOMES

NURSING HOMES
>   Nursing and personal care facilities. irreg. VIII.42.

OAKLAND, CA, PMSA
>   Census tracts. Report no. 294A. decennial. I.8.
>   Occupational compensation survey. annual. VIII.11.

OCALA, FL, MSA
>   Census tracts. Report no. 247. decennial. I.8.

OCCUPATIONS
>   Career guide to industries. annual. VIII.10A.
>   Occupational compensation survey. annual. VIII.11.
>   Occupational compensation survey. Selected metropolitan areas.
>   annual. VIII.12.
>   Occupational compensation survey. Summary. annual. VIII.13.
>   Occupational outlook handbook. biennial. VIII.15.
>   Occupations of federal white-collar and blue-collar workers. biennial.
>   VIII.4.
>   Temporary help supply. irreg. VIII.48.
>   White collar pay: private goods-producing industries. biennial.
>   VIII.52.
>   White collar pay: private service-producing industries. biennial.
>   VIII.47.
>   *see also specific occupations, e.g.,* ENGINEERS; PHYSICIANS;
>   SCIENTISTS*; and types of industries, e.g.,* EDUCATION;
>   HEALTH CARE

OCEAN, NJ *see* MONMOUTH-OCEAN, NJ, PMSA

ODESSA, TX, MSA
>Census tracts. Report no. 248. decennial. I.8.

OGDEN, UT *see* SALT LAKE CITY-OGDEN, UT, MSA

OIL INDUSTRIES
>Oil and gas extraction. irreg. VIII.34.

OKLAHOMA CITY, OK, MSA
>Census tracts. Report no. 249. decennial. I.8.
>Occupational compensation survey. Summary. annual. VIII.13.

OLYMPIA, WA, MSA
>Census tracts. Report no. 250. decennial. I.8.

OMAHA, NE-IA, MSA
>Census tracts. Report no. 251. decennial. I.8.
>Occupational compensation survey. annual. VIII.11.

ORANGE COUNTY, NY, PMSA
>Census tracts. Report no. 245K. decennial. I.8.

OREM, UT *see* PROVO-OREM, UT, MSA

ORLANDO, FL, MSA
>Census tracts. Report no. 252. decennial. I.8.
>Occupational compensation survey. annual. VIII.11.
>Occupational compensation survey. Summary. annual. VIII.13.

OSHKOSH, WI *see* APPLETON-OSHKOSH-NEENAH, WI, MSA

OWENSBORO, KY, MSA
>Census tracts. Report no. 253. decennial. I.8.

OXNARD-VENTURA, CA, PMSA
>Census tracts. Report no. 215C. decennial. I.8.
>Occupational compensation survey. Summary. annual. VIII.13.

PACIFIC-ISLANDER AMERICANS *see* ASIAN AND PACIFIC-ISLANDER
>AMERICANS

PACKING HOUSES
>Meat products. irreg. VIII.64.

PALM BAY, FL *see* MELBOURNE-TITUSVILLE-PALM BAY, FL, MSA

PANAMA
>Foreign labor trends. annual. I.24.

PANAMA CITY, FL, MSA
>Census tracts. Report no. 254. decennial. I.8.

PAPER BOX INDUSTRY
>Corrugated and solid fiber boxes. irreg. VIII.67.

PAPER INDUSTRY
>Pulp, paper, and paperboard mills. irreg. VIII.68.

PARKERSBURG-MARIETTA, WV-OH, MSA
>Census tracts. Report no. 255. decennial. I.8.

PASCAGOULA, MS, MSA
> Census tracts. Report no. 256. decennial. I.8.

PASCO, WA *see* RICHLAND-KENNEWICK-PASCO, WA, MSA

PASSAIC, NJ *see* BERGEN-PASSAIC, NJ, PMSA

PAWTUCKET-WOONSOCKET-ATTLEBORO, RI-MA, PMSA
> Census tracts. Report no. 269B. decennial. I.8.
> Occupational compensation survey. annual. VIII.11.

PENSACOLA, FL, MSA
> Census tracts. Report no. 257. decennial. I.8.

PENSIONS
> Pensions, worker coverage and retirement benefits. irreg. VII.29.
> *see also* AGED; SOCIAL INSURANCE BENEFICIARIES

PEORIA, IL, MSA
> Census tracts. Report no. 258. decennial. I.8.
> Occupational compensation survey. Summary. annual. VIII.13.

PERU
> Foreign labor trends. annual. I.24.

PETALUMA, CA *see* SANTA ROSA-PETALUMA, CA, PMSA

PETERSBURG, VA *see* RICHMOND-PETERSBURG, VA, MSA

PETROLEUM
> Petroleum refining. irreg. VIII.69.

PHILADELPHIA, PA-NJ, PMSA
> Census tracts. Report no. 259A. decennial. I.8.
> Occupational compensation survey. annual. VIII.11.

PHILADELPHIA-WILMINGTON-TRENTON, PA-NJ-DE-MD, CMSA
> Census tracts. Report nos. 259A-259D. decennial. I.8.

PHILIPPINES
> Foreign labor trends. annual. I.24.

PHOENIX, AZ, MSA
> Census tracts. Report no. 260. decennial. I.8.
> Occupational compensation survey. annual. VIII.11.

PINE BLUFF, AR, MSA
> Census tracts. Report no. 261. decennial. I.8.
> Occupational compensation survey. Summary. annual. VIII.13.

PITTSBURGH, PA, PMSA
> Census tracts. Report no. 262B. decennial. I.8.
> Occupational compensation survey. annual. VIII.11.

PITTSBURGH-BEAVER VALLEY, PA, CMSA
> Census tracts. Report nos. 262A-262B. decennial. I.8.

PITTSFIELD, MA, MSA
> Census tracts. Report no. 263. decennial. I.8.

POMPANO BEACH, FL *see* FORT LAUDERDALE-HOLLYWOOD-POMPANO
BEACH, FL, PMSA

PONCE, PR, MSA
Census tracts. Report no. 264. decennial. I.8.

POOR
Income, poverty, and wealth in the United States. irreg. VI.7.
Money income and poverty status in the United States.
annual. VI.4.
Poverty in the United States. annual. VII.28.
Social security bulletin. monthly. VII.30.
SSI recipients by state and county. annual. VII.33.

PORTERVILLE, CA *see* VISALIA-TULARE-PORTERVILLE, CA, MSA

PORTLAND, ME, MSA
Census tracts. Report no. 265. decennial. I.8.
Occupational compensation survey. annual. VIII.11.

PORTLAND, OR, PMSA
Census tracts. Report no. 266A. decennial. I.8.
Occupational compensation survey. annual. VIII.11.

PORTLAND-VANCOUVER, OR-WA, CMSA
Census tracts. Report nos. 266A-266B. decennial. I.8.

PORTSMOUTH-CHILLICOTHE-GALLIPOLIS, OH, MSA
Occupational compensation survey. Summary. annual. VIII.13.

PORTSMOUTH-DOVER-ROCHESTER, NH-ME, MSA
Census tracts. Report no. 267. decennial. I.8.

PORTUGAL
Foreign labor trends. annual. I.24.

POUGHKEEPSIE, NY, MSA
Census tracts. Report no. 268. decennial. I.8.
Occupational compensation survey. annual. VIII.11.

POUGHKEEPSIE-ORANGE COUNTY-KINGSTON AREA, NY
Occupational compensation survey. Summary. annual. VIII.13.

POVERTY *see* POOR

PROFESSIONAL EMPLOYEES
White-collar pay: private goods-producing industries.
biennial. VIII.52.
White-collar pay: private service-producing industries.
biennial. VIII.47.
see also specific professions, e.g., ENGINEERS; PHYSICIANS;
SCIENTISTS

PROVIDENCE, RI, PMSA
Census tracts. Report no. 269C. decennial. I.8.
Occupational compensation survey. Summary. annual. VIII.13.

PROVIDENCE-PAWTUCKET-FALL RIVER, RI-MA, CMSA
    Census tracts. Report nos. 269A-269C. decennial. I.8.
PROVO-OREM, UT, MSA
    Census tracts. Report no. 270. decennial. I.8.
PUBLIC SECTOR *see* GOVERNMENT
PUBLIC UTILITIES
    Electric and gas utilities. irreg. VIII.33.
PUBLIC WELFARE
    SSI recipients by state and county. annual. VII.33.
PUEBLO, CO, MSA
    Census tracts. Report no. 271. decennial. I.8.
    Occupational compensation survey. Summary. annual. VIII.13.
PUERTO RICO
    Occupational compensation survey. Summary. annual. VIII.13.
RACINE, WI, PMSA
    Census tracts. Report no. 231B. decennial. I.8.
RALEIGH-DURHAM, NC, MSA
    Census tracts. Report no. 272. decennial. I.8.
    Occupational compensation survey. Summary. annual. VIII.13.
RANTOUL, IL *see* CHAMPAIGN-URBANA-RANTOUL, IL, MSA
RAPID CITY, SD, MSA
    Census tracts. Report no. 273. decennial. I.8.
READING, PA, MSA
    Census tracts. Report no. 274. decennial. I.8.
REDDING, CA, MSA
    Census tracts. Report no. 275. decennial. I.8.
REFUGEES
    Refugee resettlement program. annual. VII.34.
RENO, NV, MSA
    Census tracts. Report no. 276. decennial. I.8.
    Occupational compensation survey. Summary. annual. VIII.13.
REPAIRING INDUSTRY
    Industry wage survey. Appliance repair. irreg. VIII.43.
RETIREES
    Pensions, worker coverage and retirement benefits. VII.29. irreg.
    see also AGED; SOCIAL INSURANCE BENEFICIARIES
RICHLAND-KENNEWICK-PASCO, WA, MSA
    Census tracts. Report no. 277. decennial. I.8.
RICHMOND-PETERSBURG, VA, MSA
    Census tracts. Report no. 278. decennial. I.8.
    Occupational compensation survey. annual. VIII.11.

RIVERSIDE-SAN BERNARDINO, CA, PMSA
>Census tracts. Report no. 215D. decennial. I.8.
>Occupational compensation survey. annual. VIII.11.

ROANOKE, VA, MSA
>Census tracts. Report no. 279. decennial. I.8.

ROCHESTER, MN, MSA
>Census tracts. Report no. 280. decennial. I.8.

ROCHESTER, NH *see* PORTSMOUTH-DOVER-ROCHESTER, NH-ME, MSA

ROCHESTER, NY, MSA
>Census tracts. Report no. 281. decennial. I.8.
>Occupational compensation survey. annual. VIII.11.

ROCK HILL, SC *see* CHARLOTTE-GASTONIA-ROCK HILL, NC-SC, MSA

ROCK ISLAND, IL *see* DAVENPORT-ROCK ISLAND-MOLINE, IA-IL,
>MSA

ROCKFORD, IL, MSA
>Census tracts. Report no. 282. decennial. I.8.

ROME, NY *see* UTICA-ROME, NY, MSA

SACRAMENTO, CA, MSA
>Census tracts. Report no. 283. decennial. I.8.

SAGINAW-BAY CITY-MIDLAND, MI, MSA
>Census tracts. Report no. 284. decennial. I.8.
>Occupational compensation survey. Summary. annual. VIII.13.

ST. CLOUD, MN, MSA
>Census tracts. Report no. 285. decennial. I.8.
>Occupational compensation survey. annual. VIII.11.

ST. JOSEPH, MO, MSA
>Census tracts. Report no. 286. decennial. I.8.

ST. LOUIS, MO-IL, MSA
>Census tracts. Report no. 287. decennial. I.8.
>Occupational compensation survey. annual. VIII.11.

ST. PAUL, MN *see* MINNEAPOLIS-ST. PAUL, MN-WI, MSA

ST. PETERSBURG, FL *see* TAMPA-ST. PETERSBURG-CLEARWATER, FL,
>MSA

SALEM, OR, MSA
>Census tracts. Report no. 288. decennial. I.8.

SALEM-GLOUCESTER, MA, PMSA
>Census tracts. Report no. 95F. decennial. I.8.

SALINA, KS, MSA
>Occupational compensation survey. Summary. annual. VIII.13.

SANTA ROSA-PETALUMA, CA, PMSA
> Census tracts. Report no. 294E. decennial. I.8.

SARASOTA, FL, MSA
> Census tracts. Report no. 298. decennial. I.8.

SAVANNAH, GA, MSA
> Census tracts. Report no. 299. decennial. I.8.
> Occupational compensation survey. Summary. annual. VIII.13.

SCHENECTADY, NY *see* ALBANY-SCHENECTADY-TROY, NY, MSA

SCIENCE AND TECHNOLOGY
> Science and engineering indicators. biennial. VIII.45.
> Women and minorities in science and engineering. biennial. VIII.46.

SCIENTISTS
> Characteristics of doctoral scientists and engineers in the U.S. biennial.
> VIII.44.

SCRANTON-WILKES-BARRE, PA, MSA
> Census tracts. Report no. 300. decennial. I.8.
> Occupational compensation survey. annual. VIII.11.

SEASIDE, CA *see* SALINAS-SEASIDE-MONTEREY, CA, MSA

SEATTLE, WA, PMSA
> Census tracts. Report no. 301A. decennial. I.8.
> Occupational compensation survey. annual. VIII.11.

SEATTLE-TACOMA, WA, CMSA
> Census tracts. Report nos. 301A-301B. decennial. I.8.

SELMA, AL, MSA
> Occupational compensation survey. Summary. annual. VIII.13.

SENEGAL
> Foreign labor trends. annual. I.24.

SERVICE INDUSTRIES
> Employment, hours, and earnings, United States, 1909-94. irreg. I.17.
> White-collar pay: private service-producing industries biennial.
> VIII.47.

SHARON, PA, MSA
> Census tracts. Report no. 302. decennial. I.8.

SHEBOYGAN, WI, MSA
> Census tracts. Report no. 303. decennial. I.8.

SHERIFFS
> Sheriffs' departments. triennial. VIII.39.

SHERMAN-DENISON, TX, MSA
> Census tracts. Report no. 304. decennial. I.8.

SHIPBUILDING INDUSTRY
> Report on survey of U.S. shipbuilding and repair facilities. annual.

VIII.70.

Shipbuilding and repairing. irreg. VIII.71.

SHOE INDUSTRY

Men's and women's footwear. irreg. VIII.72.

SHREVEPORT, LA, MSA

Census tracts. Report no. 305. decennial. I.8.

Occupational compensation survey. annual. VIII.11.

Occupational compensation survey. Summary. annual. VIII.13.

SINGAPORE

Foreign labor trends. annual. I.24.

SIOUX CITY, IA-NE, MSA

Census tracts. Report no. 306. decennial. I.8.

SIOUX FALLS, SD, MSA

Census tracts. Report no. 307. decennial. I.8.

SOCIAL ASSISTANCE RECIPIENTS

Social security bulletin. monthly. VII.30.

Social security bulletin, annual statistical supplement. annual. VII.32.

SSI recipients by state and county. annual. VII.33.

SOCIAL INSURANCE BENEFICIARIES

OASDI beneficiaries by state and county. annual. VII.31.

Social security bulletin. monthly. VII.30.

Social security bulletin, annual statistical supplement. annual. VII.32.

see also PENSIONS

SOMERSET, NJ *see* MIDDLESEX-SOMERSET-HUNTERDON, NJ, PMSA

SOUTH AFRICA

Foreign labor trends. annual. I.24.

SOUTH BEND-MISHAWAKA, IN, MSA

Census tracts. Report no. 308. decennial. I.8.

SOUTH DAKOTA

Occupational compensation survey. Summary. annual. VIII.13.

SPARTANBURG, SC *see* GREENVILLE-SPARTANBURG, SC, MSA

SPOKANE, WA, MSA

Census tracts. Report no. 309. decennial. I.8.

Occupational compensation survey. Summary. annual. VIII.13.

SPRINGDALE, AR *see* FAYETTEVILLE-SPRINGDALE, AR, MSA

SPRINGFIELD, IL, MSA

Census tracts. Report no. 310. decennial. I.8.

Occupational compensation survey. Summary. annual. VIII.13.

SPRINGFIELD, MA, MSA

Census tracts. Report no. 312. decennial. I.8.

SPRINGFIELD, MO, MSA
    Census tracts. Report no. 311. decennial. I.8.
SPRINGFIELD, OH *see* DAYTON-SPRINGFIELD, OH, MSA
SPRINGFIELD, OR *see* EUGENE-SPRINGFIELD, OR, MSA
STAMFORD, CT, PMSA
    Census tracts. Report no. 245L. decennial. I.8.
STATE COLLEGE, PA, MSA
    Census tracts. Report no. 313. decennial. I.8.
STATE DATA *see* UNITED STATES—NATIONAL, STATES *and other*
    subdivisions under UNITED STATES
STEEL INDUSTRY
    Basic iron and steel. irreg. VIII.74.
    Iron and steel foundries. irreg. VIII.75.
    Quarterly report on the status of the steel industry. quarterly. VIII.73.
STEUBENVILLE-WEIRTON, OH-WV, MSA
    Census tracts. Report no. 314. decennial. I.8.
STOCKTON, CA, MSA
    Census tracts. Report no. 315. decennial. I.8.
    Occupational compensation survey. Summary. annual. VIII.13.
SUFFOLK, NY *see* NASSAU-SUFFOLK, NY, PMSA
SURINAME
    Foreign labor trends. annual. I.24.
SWEDEN
    Foreign labor trends. annual. I.24.
SWITZERLAND
    Foreign labor trends. annual. I.24.
SYRACUSE, NY, MSA
    Census tracts. Report no. 316. decennial. I.8.
TACOMA, WA, PMSA
    Census tracts. Report no. 301B. decennial. I.8.
    Occupational compensation survey. Summary. annual. VIII.13.
TAIWAN
    Foreign labor trends. annual. I.24.
TALLAHASSEE, FL, MSA
    Census tracts. Report no. 317. decennial. I.8.
TAMPA-ST. PETERSBURG-CLEARWATER, FL, MSA
    Census tracts. Report no. 318. decennial. I.8.
TAMPA-ST. PETERSBURG, FL, MSA (as defined by BLS)
    Occupational compensation survey. Summary. annual. VIII.13.
TEACHERS *see* EDUCATION
TECHNOLOGY *see* SCIENCE AND TECHNOLOGY

TEMPLE, TX *see* KILLEEN-TEMPLE, TX, MSA
TEMPORARY EMPLOYMENT
Temporary help supply. irreg. VIII.48.
TERRE HAUTE, IN, MSA
Census tracts. Report no. 319. decennial. I.8.
TEXARKANA, TX-TEXARKANA, AR, MSA
Census tracts. Report no. 320. decennial. I.8.
TEXAS CITY, TX *see* GALVESTON-TEXAS CITY, TX, PMSA
TEXAS, NORTHWEST
Occupational compensation survey. Summary. annual. VIII.13.
TEXTILE INDUSTRY
Synthetic fibers. irreg. VIII.76.
Textile plants. irreg. VIII.77.
THAILAND
Foreign labor trends. annual. I.24.
THIBODAUX, LA *see* HOUMA-THIBODAUX, LA, MSA
TITUSVILLE, TX *see* MELBOURNE-TITUSVILLE-PALM BAY, FL, MSA
TOBACCO *see* CIGARETTE INDUSTRY
TOLEDO, OH, MSA
Census tracts. Report no. 321. decennial. I.8.
Occupational compensation survey. annual. VIII.11.
TOPEKA, KS, MSA
Census tracts. Report no. 322. decennial. I.8.
Occupational compensation survey. Summary. annual. VIII.13.
TRADE UNION WORKERS
News. Union members. annual. VII.35.
TRANSPORTATION
National transportation statistics. annual. VIII.49.
TRENTON, NJ, PMSA
Census tracts. Report no. 259B. decennial. I.8.
Occupational compensation survey. annual. VIII.11.
TRINIDAD AND TOBAGO
Foreign labor trends. annual. I.24.
TROY, NY *see* ALBANY-SCHENECTADY-TROY, NY, MSA
TUCSON, AZ, MSA
Census tracts. Report no. 323. decennial. I.8.
TUCSON-DOUGLAS, AZ, MSA
Occupational compensation survey. Summary. annual. VIII.13.
TULARE, CA *see* VISALIA-TULARE-PORTERVILLE, CA, MSA

UNITED STATES—COUNTIES/METROPOLITAN AREAS, CITIES, LOCAL
    AREAS
    Census tracts. decennial. I.8.
UNITED STATES—METROPOLITAN AREAS
    Census of population. Social and economic characteristics. Metropolitan
        areas. decennial. I.13.
    Occupational compensation survey. annual. VIII.11.
    Occupational compensation survey. Selected metropolitan areas.
        annual. VIII.12.
    Occupational compensation survey. Summary. annual. VIII.13.
UNITED STATES—NATIONAL, STATES
    Employment and wages, annual averages. annual. I.4.
    Handbook of labor statistics. annual. I.19.
    State personal income 1929-(yr.). irreg. VI.8.
    Statistical abstract of the United States. annual. I.5
    .Survey of current business. monthly. I.22.
UNITED STATES—NATIONAL, STATES, COUNTIES/METROPOLITAN
    AREAS
    Employment and earnings. monthly. I.1.
    Local area personal income. annual. VI.3.
    U.S.A. counties, a statistical abstract supplement. annual. I.7.
UNITED STATES—NATIONAL, STATES, COUNTIES/METROPOLITAN
    AREAS, CITIES
    County and city data book. quinquennial. I.15.
    Social and economic characteristics. decennial. I.12.
    Summary social, economic, and housing characteristics. decennial.   I.10.
    Summary tape file (STF) 3C. decennial. I.11.
UNITED STATES—STATES, COUNTIES/METROPOLITAN AREAS, CITIES
    Local population estimates. biennial. VI.6.
    Regional economic information system. annual. VI.5A.
    State and metropolitan area data book. irreg. I.27.
UNITED STATES—STATES, METROPOLITAN AREAS
    Employment, hours, and earnings, states and areas, 1987-92. irreg.   I.16.
UNITED STATES—ZIP CODES
    Summary tape file (STF) 3B. decennial. I.11.
UPPER PENINSULA, MI, MSA
    Occupational compensation survey. Summary. annual. VIII.13.
URBANA, IL *see* CHAMPAIGN-URBANA-RANTOUL, IL, MSA
URUGUAY
    Foreign labor trends. annual. I.24.
USSR
    Foreign labor trends. annual. I.24.

UTICA-ROME, NY, MSA
    Census tracts. Report no. 327. decennial. I.8.
UTILITIES *see* PUBLIC UTILITIES
VALLEJO-FAIRFIELD-NAPA, CA, PMSA
    Census tracts. Report no. 294F. decennial. I.8.
    Occupational compensation survey. Summary. annual. VIII.13.
VANCOUVER, WA, PMSA
    Census tracts. Report no. 266B. decennial. I.8.
VENTURA, CA *see* OXNARD-VENTURA, CA, PMSA
VERMONT
    Occupational compensation survey. Summary. annual. VIII.13.
VICTORIA, TX, MSA
    Census tracts. Report no. 328. decennial. I.8.
VINELAND-MILLVILLE-BRIDGETON, NJ, PMSA
    Census tracts. Report no. 259C. decennial. I.8.
VIRGIN ISLANDS OF THE U.S.
    Occupational compensation survey. Summary. annual. VIII.13.
VIRGINIA BEACH *see* NORFOLK-VIRGINIA BEACH-NEWPORT NEWS,
    VA, MSA
VIRGINIA, SOUTHWEST
    Occupational compensation survey. Summary. annual. VIII.13.
VISALIA-TULARE-PORTERVILLE, CA, MSA
    Census tracts. Report no. 329. decennial. I.8.
    Occupational compensation survey. annual. VIII.11.
WACO, TX, MSA
    Census tracts. Report no. 330. decennial. I.8.
WARNER ROBINS, GA *see* MACON-WARNER ROBINS, GA, MSA
WARREN, OH *see* YOUNGSTOWN-WARREN, OH, MSA
WASHINGTON, DC-MD-VA, MSA
    Census tracts. Report no. 331. decennial. I.8.
    Occupational compensation survey. annual. VIII.11.
WATERBURY, CT, MSA
    Census tracts. Report no. 332. decennial. I.8.
WATERLOO-CEDAR FALLS, IA, MSA
    Census tracts. Report no. 333. decennial. I.8.
    Occupational compensation survey. Summary. annual. VIII.13.
WAUSAU, WI, MSA
    Census tracts. Report no. 334. decennial. I.8.
WEALTH
    Income, poverty, and wealth in the United States: a chartbook. irreg.
        VI.7.

WEIRTON, WV *see* STEUBENVILLE-WEIRTON, OH-WV, MSA

WELFARE *see* PUBLIC WELFARE

WEST PALM BEACH-BOCA RATON-DELRAY BEACH, FL, MSA
>Census tracts. Report no. 335. decennial. I.8.

WEST VIRGINIA
>Occupational compensation survey. Summary. annual. VIII.13.

WHEELING, WV-OH, MSA
>Census tracts. Report no. 336. decennial. I.8.

WHITE-COLLAR WORKERS
>Occupations of federal white-collar and blue-collar workers. VIII.4.
>White-collar pay: private goods-producing industries. biennial.
>VIII.52.
>White-collar pay: private service-producing industries. biennial.
>VIII.47.

WICHITA FALLS, TX, MSA
>Census tracts. Report no. 338. decennial. I.8.

WICHITA, KS, MSA
>Census tracts. Report no. 337. decennial. I.8.
>Occupational compensation survey. Summary. annual. VIII.13.

WILKES-BARRE, PA *see* SCRANTON-WILKES-BARRE, PA, MSA

WILLIAMSPORT, PA, MSA
>Census tracts. Report no. 339. decennial. I.8.

WILMINGTON, DE-NJ-MD, MSA
>Occupational compensation survey. annual. VIII.11.
>Occupational compensation survey. Summary. annual. VIII.13.

WILMINGTON, DE-NJ-MD, PMSA
>Census tracts. Report no. 259D. decennial. I.8.
>Occupational compensation survey. annual. VIII.11.
>Occupational compensation survey. Summary. annual. VIII.13.

WILMINGTON, NC, MSA
>Census tracts. Report no. 340. decennial. I.8.

WINSTON-SALEM, NC *see* GREENSBORO-WINSTON-SALEM-HIGH POINT,
NC, MSA

WINTER HAVEN, FL *see* LAKELAND-WINTER HAVEN, FL, MSA

WOMEN
>Annual report on the employment of minorities, women, and people with
>disabilities in the federal government. annual. VIII.1.
>Facts on working women. irreg. VII.17.
>Job patterns for minorities and women in state and local government.
>annual. VIII.8.
>We the American...women. decennial. VII.16.
>Women and minorities in science and engineering. biennial. VIII.46.

Women & work. monthly. VII.15.
Working women: a chartbook. irreg. VII.18.
WOODWORK AND WOODWORKERS *see* MILLWORK
WOONSOCKET, RI *see* PAWTUCKET-WOONSOCKET-ATTLEBORO, RI-MA, PMSA
WORCESTER, MA, MSA
    Census tracts. Report no. 341. decennial. I.8.
    Occupational compensation survey. annual. VIII.11.
WORKER RIGHTS—DEVELOPING COUNTRIES
    Foreign labor trends. annual. I.24.
WORKER RIGHTS—EASTERN EUROPE
    Foreign labor trends. annual. I.24.
WORKER RIGHTS—UNITED STATES—FOREIGN POLICY
    Foreign labor trends. annual. I.24.
YAKIMA, WA, MSA
    Census tracts. Report no. 342. decennial. I.8.
YAKIMA-RICHLAND-KENNEWICK-PASCO-WALLA WALLA-PENDLETON AREA, WA-OR
    Occupational compensation survey. Summary. annual. VIII.13.
YORK, PA, MSA
    Census tracts. Report no. 343. decennial. I.8.
    Occupational compensation survey. annual. VIII.11.
YOUNGSTOWN-WARREN, OH, MSA
    Census tracts. Report no. 344. decennial. I.8.
YOUTH
    Youth indicators: trends in the well being of American youth. irreg. VII.36.
YUBA CITY, CA, MSA
    Census tracts. Report no. 345. decennial. I.8.
YUGOSLAVIA
    Foreign labor trends. annual. I.24.
YUMA, AZ, MSA
    Census tracts. Report no. 346. decennial. I.8.
ZAIRE
    Foreign labor trends. annual. I.24.
ZIMBABWE
    Foreign labor trends. annual. I.24.

About the Author

John M. Ross (MLS, University of Southern California), was documents librarian at the University Library, California State University, Los Angeles, from 1962-1992. He is the author of *National Criminal Justice Reference Service (NCJRS) Bibliographies: a Bibliography of Bibliographies*; *Foreign Trade Publications in U.S. Documents: a Selective Bibliography*; and *How to Use the Major Indexes to U.S. Government Publications*. He is also the author of *Trials in Collections: an Index to Famous Trials throughout the World.*